Nationalising the Crusades

Engaging the Crusades is a series of concise volumes (up to 50,000 words) which offer initial windows into the ways in which the crusades have been used in the last two centuries, demonstrating that the memory of the crusades is an important and emerging subject. Together these studies suggest that the memory of the crusades, in the modern period, is a productive, exciting, and much needed area of investigation.

Despite their 'intrinsic internationalism', the crusades have long been conscripted for nationalist ends. The last decade has seen an upsurge in usage of the crusades to justify and inspire violence played out within and across national contexts. This volume furthers study of nationalist uses of the crusades and crusading by broadening the focus of study beyond north-western Europe and by showcasing different approaches to illustrate how the memory of the crusades has been employed within and between nations. This takes the form of tightly focused case studies and broader overviews covering the ambivalent role of foreign crusaders in Portuguese commemorations of the battle of Lisbon in 1947, Russian holy war rhetoric and theology, Zionist perceptions of the crusader castle of 'Athlit, the role of individuals as 'cultural brokers' of crusader heritage amidst European imperial competition, and how crusading as a part of European medievalism was received and reflected in Japan in the late nineteenth and early twentieth centuries.

This book will be of interest to scholars and students considering national identity, medievalism, and religious violence and to those with specific interest in the contexts of each chapter.

Mike Horswell is a fellow of the Royal Historical Society and has a doctorate from Royal Holloway. He is the founder and co-series editor of *Engaging the Crusades;* he researches, teaches, and has published work on the modern memory and legacy of the crusades and is the author of *The Rise and Fall of British Crusader Medievalism, c.1825–1945* (2018).

ENGAGING THE CRUSADES

THE MEMORY AND LEGACY OF CRUSADING

SERIES EDITORS
JONATHAN PHILLIPS AND MIKE HORSWELL

Engaging the Crusades
The Memory and Legacy of Crusading
Series Editors: Jonathan Phillips and Mike Horswell
Royal Holloway, University of London, UK

Engaging the Crusades is a series of volumes which offer initial windows into the ways in which the crusades have been used in the last two centuries, demonstrating that the memory of the crusades is an important and emerging subject. Together these studies suggest that the memory of the crusades, in the modern period, is a productive, exciting, and much needed area of investigation.
  In this series:

The Making of Crusading Heroes and Villains
Engaging the Crusades, Volume Four
Edited by Mike Horswell and Kristin Skottki

Playing the Crusades
Engaging the Crusades, Volume Five
Edited by Robert Houghton

Tales of the Crusaders – Remembering the Crusades in Britain
Engaging the Crusades, Volume Six
Elizabeth Siberry

The Modern Memory of the Military-religious Orders
Engaging the Crusades, Volume Seven
Edited by Rory MacLellan

Nationalising the Crusades
Engaging the Crusades, Volume Eight
Edited by Mike Horswell

For more information about this series, please visit: https://www.routledge.com/Engaging-the-Crusades/book-series/ETC

Nationalising the Crusades
Engaging the Crusades, Volume Eight

Edited by Mike Horswell

LONDON AND NEW YORK

First published 2023
by Routledge
4 Park Square, Milton Park, Abingdon, Oxon OX14 4RN

and by Routledge
605 Third Avenue, New York, NY 10158

Routledge is an imprint of the Taylor & Francis Group, an informa business

© 2023 selection and editorial matter, Mike Horswell; individual chapters, the contributors

The right of Mike Horswell to be identified as the author of the editorial material, and of the authors for their individual chapters, has been asserted in accordance with sections 77 and 78 of the Copyright, Designs and Patents Act 1988.

All rights reserved. No part of this book may be reprinted or reproduced or utilised in any form or by any electronic, mechanical, or other means, now known or hereafter invented, including photocopying and recording, or in any information storage or retrieval system, without permission in writing from the publishers.

Trademark notice: Product or corporate names may be trademarks or registered trademarks, and are used only for identification and explanation without intent to infringe.

British Library Cataloguing-in-Publication Data
A catalogue record for this book is available from the British Library

ISBN: 978-1-032-14954-7 (hbk)
ISBN: 978-1-032-14955-4 (pbk)
ISBN: 978-1-003-24193-5 (ebk)

DOI: 10.4324/9781003241935

Typeset in Times New Roman
by KnowledgeWorks Global Ltd.

Contents

List of Figures viii
Acknowledgements ix
List of Abbreviations x
List of Contributors xi

Introduction: Crusade and Nation 1
MIKE HORSWELL

1 **'Heroes and Martyrs'?: National Memories and Foreign Crusaders in Portuguese Commemorations of the Eighth Centenary of the Conquest of Lisbon (1947)** 21
PEDRO MARTINS

2 **The Tsar's Crusade: Invented Holy War Tradition in Russia (1780–1920)** 45
ADAM KNOBLER

3 **Perceptions of Crusader 'Athlit in Zionist Writing (1887–1941)** 58
JUDITH BRONSTEIN

4 **Cultural Brokers in the Nationalisation of Crusader Architecture** 76
ASTRID SWENSON

5 **Bushido, Chivalry, and the Crusades in Japan from the 1870s to the First World War** 98
OLEG BENESCH

Index 122

Figures

0.1 Glyn Warren Philpot, 'Richard I Leaving for the Crusade 1189', c.1926, St Stephen's Hall, Houses of Parliament, London   2
1.1 The beginning of the *Cortejo do Mundo Português* (Pageant of the Portuguese World) at the *Exposição do Mundo Português*, 1940   25
1.2 'King Afonso Henriques' surrounded by the crusaders at the *Cortejo Histórico de Lisboa*, 6 July 1947   33
1.3 Cover of the booklet containing the official programme of the centenary, designed by Manuel Lapa   34
1.4 Cover of the children's book by Leyguarda Ferreira, *A conquista de Lisboa aos Mouros* (Lisboa: Romano Torres, 1947). Design by Litografia Amorim   34
1.5 Official poster of the centenary   35
1.6 Official poster of the centenary   35
1.7 Official poster of the centenary   36
1.8 Commemorative medal of the centenary, designed by the sculptor Álvaro de Brée   36
2.1 Tsar Nicholas II in the guise of a *bogatyr*; 'Holy War', 1914   49
3.1 'Ruins of a Castle at Atlit', Z. Kluger, 1937/38   59
5.1 'Japanese warriors and religion' depicting the medieval warlord Katō Kiyomasa (1562–1611) in front of a Buddhist banner with a chant of devotion to the Lotus Sutra ('*Namu Myōhō Renge Kyō*'), from Takagi Takeshi's 1915 book *Comparing Eastern and Western Bushidō*   105
5.2 'Western warriors and religion', from Takagi Takeshi's 1915 book *Comparing Eastern and Western Bushidō*   106

Acknowledgements

The making of this volume of *Engaging the Crusades* has been a longer task than many of the others due to the myriad challenges posed by the COVID-19 pandemic. While three of the essays originate from the original *Engaging the Crusades* conference in London in 2015, three others have been written or adapted for the volume. All the authors have exhibited considerable patience, commitment, and good humour amidst the disruption of the pandemic, and the final publication is a tribute to these qualities.

I would like to thank – in no particular order – Jonathan Phillips, Felix Hinz, Kristin Skottki, Thomas Simpson, Aleks Pluskowski, Roy van Zitteren, and the reviewers of the proposal for various advice and assistance in its production as well as Laura Pilsworth and Isabel Voice at Routledge for overseeing publication.

The eighth volume of *Engaging the Crusades* sees the series into its fifth year of publication. Showcasing the variety and vitality of the subject, it has included two book length studies and seven essay collections; the latter have included over 35 chapters on aspects of the modern uses of the crusades and military orders. It has included field-leading contributions from senior academics, early career researchers, independent scholars, and graduate students and has made steps towards including pieces from a broad range of contexts. Reflecting the attention that medievalism in general, and the uses of the crusades in particular, are attracting, the series has begun what we hoped in establishing it, namely providing a home for the subject and catalysing new work in the field. There remains a need for a greater diversity of perspective, both in terms of content and contributors, and the editors would welcome proposals for volumes for the series which would add to its range and develop the field.

Finally, my thanks as always to Lauren for the countless ways in which you have facilitated this volume seeing the light of day and to my parents Ian and Rosie for their long support and encouragement.

Abbreviations

CUP   Cambridge University Press
MUP Manchester University Press
OUP Oxford University Press

Frequently used references:

Knobler, 'Holy Wars'	Knobler, Adam, 'Holy Wars, Empires, and the Portability of the Past: The Modern Uses of Medieval Crusades', *Comparative Studies in Society and History* 48 (2006), pp. 293–325.
Horswell, *British Crusader Medievalism*	Horswell, Mike, *The Rise and Fall of British Crusader Medievalism, c. 1825–1945*. Abingdon: Routledge, 2018.
Engaging the Crusades, Vol. 1	Horswell, Mike and Phillips, Jonathan, eds., *Perceptions of the Crusades from the Nineteenth to the Twenty-First Century: Engaging the Crusades, Volume One*. Abingdon: Routledge, 2018.
Engaging the Crusades, Vol. 2	Horswell, Mike and Awan, Akil. N., eds., *The Crusades in the Modern World: Engaging the Crusades, Volume Two*. Abingdon: Routledge, 2020.
Siberry, *New Crusaders*	Siberry, Elizabeth, *The New Crusaders: Images of the Crusades in the 19th and Early 20th Centuries*. Aldershot: Ashgate, 2000.
Tyerman, *Debate*	Tyerman, Christopher, *The Debate on the Crusades*. Manchester: MUP, 2011.

Contributors

Oleg Benesch is Professor of East Asian History at the University of York. His publications include *Inventing the Way of the Samurai: Nationalism, Internationalism, and Bushido in Modern Japan* (Oxford, 2014) and, with Ran Zwigenberg, *Japan's Castles: Citadels of Modernity in War and Peace* (Cambridge, 2019). For more information on his research, please see www.olegbenesch.com.

Judith Bronstein is a senior lecturer at the Department of Israel Studies, University of Haifa. Her research focuses on the history of the Military Orders in the Middle Ages, the crusade movement, and the Latin East. Among her publications are *The Hospitallers and the Holy Land; Financing the Latin East, 1187–1274* and *Settlement and Crusade in the 13th Century: Multidisciplinary Studies of the Latin East* (co-edited with Gil Fishhof and Vardit Shotten-Hallel) as well as numerous articles in academic collections and journals. She is currently working on the relation between food and culture in the Latin Kingdom of Jerusalem. Her research interests also extend to the study of modern perceptions of the crusades.

Adam Knobler, apl Professor of Religious Studies at Ruhr Universität Bochum, has published widely in the fields of crusader medievalism and early modern European imperial expansion. His monograph, *Mythology and Diplomacy in the Age of Exploration* (Leiden: Brill, 2016), concerned the uses of medieval mythology in Early modern Iberian expansion. He has a forthcoming monograph from Routledge on the global uses of crusading imagery and rhetoric in the long nineteenth century and is also working on a jointly authored study on the Ten Lost Tribes of Israel in Jewish, Christian, and Muslim thought, under contract with Oxford University Press.

xii *Contributors*

Mike Horswell completed his PhD in 2017 at Royal Holloway, University of London, and his book – *The Rise and Fall of British Crusader Medievalism, c. 1825–1945* – was published by Routledge in 2018. A founding editor of the *Engaging the Crusades* series, he is also the author of several articles and book chapters and his work includes studies of crusading in the *Encyclopaedia Britannica* and Wikipedia, the 1999 Reconciliation Walk, and crusading imagery in digital games; he has forthcoming work considering reception studies, teaching medievalism, historiography, and crusader statues. He has taught at Royal Holloway, King's College London, the University of Oxford, and the University of Bayreuth and is a Fellow of the Royal Historical Society.

Pedro Alexandre Guerreiro Martins is an Integrated Researcher at the Instituto de História Contemporânea – Faculdade de Ciências Sociais e Humanas da Universidade NOVA de Lisboa / IN2PAST — Laboratório Associado para a Investigação e Inovação em Património, Artes, Sustentabilidade e Território (IHC – NOVA FCSH / IN2PAST). He graduated in History and completed a master's degree in Modern and Contemporary History at the same faculty. In 2016, he completed a joint PhD with the University of Lucerne (Switzerland) with a dissertation on the representations of the medieval past in Portugal between the late nineteenth and the early twentieth century. He is currently working at IHC's publisher, Imprensa de História Contemporânea. He is also the editorial director of *Práticas da História: Journal on Theory, Historiography and Uses of the Past.*

Astrid Swenson is Professor of European Historical Cultures at the University of Bayreuth in Germany, having previously taught in Cambridge, London, and Bath. She writes on heritage, memory, art, and museums in Modern Europe from a transnational and transimperial perspective. Her publications include *The Rise of Heritage in France, Germany and England, 1789–1914* (Cambridge University Press, 2013), *From Plunder to Preservation: Britain and the Heritage of Empire* (edited with Peter Mandler, Oxford University Press, 2013), and *Art Looting and Restitution in the 20th Century* (Special issue of the *Journal of Contemporary History* 2017 edited with Bianca Gaudenzi). She is currently working on a book provisionally titled *Crusader Heritages: Architecture and Imperialism in the Modern Mediterranean.*

Introduction
Crusade and Nation

Mike Horswell

Introduction

In St Stephen's Hall in the Houses of Parliament in London hangs a painting of King Richard I, 'the Lionheart' departing for the Third Crusade (1189–92) as part of a series depicting foundational events in British history.[1] Glyn Philpot's piece – commissioned by a committee led by the educator and advocate of wartime chivalry Sir Henry Newbolt – sits alongside images of King Alfred's navy defeating the Danes, the signing of the Magna Carta by King John, and the Union of Scotland and England, among other episodes. In its principal figure it also evokes Baron Marochetti's triumphal statue of Richard which has stood since 1861 outside the building. The paintings were unveiled by Prime Minister Stanley Baldwin on 28 June 1927, when he declared the intention of the scenes was to be a narration of national history: 'the idea of the whole scheme [...] was the idea of how we in this country came to be what we are.'[2] Newbolt's presentation of the painting quoted the historian G.M. Trevelyan who linked the crusades with imperial expansion, arguing that the crusades 'were the first phase in that outward thrust of the restless and energetic races of the new Europe, which was never to cease until it had overrun the globe'.[3] But the national connection between the crusades and the British contained incongruity: the crusades were seen almost exclusively through Richard; Richard was an English or Angevin (not British) king; and his venture was unsuccessful. Indeed, Baldwin commented of Philpot's scene that 'We shall see Cœur de Lion starting off on one of those crusades which, in common with so much human endeavour, started in impulses of idealism and led to the breaking of all ideals and to disaster.'[4] Regardless, in the inauguration of the installation of the paintings in 1927 the crusades were being incorporated into a British national story and celebrated at the seat of government (Fig. 0.1).

DOI: 10.4324/9781003241935-1

2 *Mike Horswell*

Figure 0.1 Glyn Warren Philpot, 'Richard I Leaving for the Crusade 1189', c.1926, St Stephen's Hall, Houses of Parliament, London.
Source: Henry Newbolt, *The Building of Britain* (London: 1927).

The quintessential example of national uses of the crusades and crusading are at the Palace of Versailles in France. In 1833 the French king Louis Philippe commenced the refurbishment of the Palace as a monument to past glory for the troubled nation. Created in the renovation were the Salle des Croisades, a series of rooms containing over 120 portraits and paintings of triumphant events in the history of the crusades and the Hospitaller knights.[5] These were paralleled with the expedition of Charles X to North Africa in the 1840s and designed to visually impress on viewers the long and glorious history of French military intervention overseas. 'We must not forget', wrote the late medievalist Jean Richard of the crusading rooms, 'that the intention was to recall the glories of France; the exploits of the Franks in the Holy Land were assimilated to those of the French of France.'[6] Moreover, with the inclusion of the arms of those whose ancestors had participated in the crusades Louis Philippe further entwined the crusading past with the royalist present. The desire of aristocratic families to discover a crusading ancestor, and thereby secure the inclusion of their family arms in the rooms, famously led to a vibrant industry forging medieval documentation.[7] It also neatly illustrates some of the ways in which memories of the crusades and crusading can and could be re-narrated and re-presented for nationalist ends.

'Nationalism is back if it ever disappeared' begins a survey published in 2021 of 'new' nationalism in the twenty-first century.[8] The re-emergence of nationalist rhetoric around the world, coupled with appropriations of the crusades, represents a pressing contemporary concern; in particular the recent trend for the crusades to be invoked to justify and further incite acts of violence, especially by far-right white supremacists. These are ostensibly internationalist groups – who cite a shared white, Christian, Western European, civilisational heritage and culture under attack – and yet the application is often narrowly nationalist. In the early twenty-first century, Anders Breivik's neo-Templar identity was applied to an attack on a Norwegian political party's youth in 2011; it was framed as a local response of an international group (Breivik's imagined neo-Templar, trans-European brotherhood) targeting political 'enemies' to Norwegian multiculturalism.[9] The English Defence League has employed a modified Templar logo, while at both the far-right rally at Charlottesville in the US in August 2017 and in the storming of the Capitol building in January 2021 a few participants displayed crusading – often Templar – symbols. Again, in these cases the international Templars have been adopted for nationalist ends.[10] The mosque shootings in Christchurch, New Zealand, in March 2019 were conducted by shooter who referenced the First Crusader Bohemond of Taranto on his weapon.[11] The battle cry of the Templars, 'Deus Vult!', has become part-internet meme, part-rallying cry of the far-right while neo-Templar orders – some more violent than others – have sprung up in recent years.[12] In Brazil, supporters of Jair Bolsonaro have emphasised a European past as the 'true' heritage of the nation, often employing 'Deus Vult'; the online 2017 historical documentary series by Brasil Paralelo, viewed over 3.5 million times on YouTube, is titled 'Brazil – The Last Crusade'.[13] The rise of Islamic State (IS/ISIS/ISIL/Daesh) in the first two decades of the twenty-first century saw jihadis attempt to create their own Middle Eastern nation-state, using opposition to a constructed homogeneity of 'Western Crusaders' (medieval and modern) as an antithesis. Members performed horrific acts of violence such as beheadings which were staged for media impact, retransmission and to inspire further atrocities. The rhetoric of universal religious conflict of which crusading was a part transcends national boundaries; couching their propaganda in these broad terms has enabled groups to connect with causes from around the world despite, for instance, the specific state-building aims of IS.[14]

This volume takes seriously nationalised perspectives on crusading – not as immanent, inevitable categories which define the reality of the crusading movement, but as powerful, contingent ways of viewing the past. One of the tasks of investigating crusader medievalism is to write the past of these perceptions, showing that they have a history, how they are constructed and to what ends they are put, in order to explode the idea that they supply inalienable justification for these uses. Approaching the memory and uses of the crusades through national lenses reveals the ways that thinking nationally has shaped our understanding of the crusades today, as well as in the past.

In the light of nationalist deployments of the crusades this volume seeks to broaden analyses of these uses in two dimensions. Firstly, it builds on work on France and Britain by moving the focus of study to the north-eastern periphery of Europe, to either end of the Mediterranean, and to reflections in a Japanese mirror. Secondly, and crucially, rather than merely adding further national perspectives on the crusades as a whole, contributions to this volume offer additional insight into particular *ways* in which these national uses of the medieval past are employed and play out. Pedro Martins' tight case study of a Portuguese crusading anniversary in 1947 illustrates the political uses of commemoration and its constructed nature through the flexible presentation (or absence) of foreign crusaders. Adam Knobler's chapter presents a long view of Russian engagement with crusading and holy war, drawing out its flexibility and reappropriation. Judith Bronstein considers the ways in which collective memory bends around extant material architecture of the past through connecting changing perceptions of the Templar castle at 'Athlit with successive stages of Zionist settlement. Astrid Swenson builds on her work on crusader heritage by here highlighting the role of individuals as 'cultural brokers' negotiating roles within and between nations in the Eastern Mediterranean in the first half of the twentieth century. Finally, Oleg Benesch offers a tantalising glimpse of the reception of the crusades by the Japanese as part of a reflection and internalising of British chivalric medievalism, resulting in the creation of bushido, the 'way of the samurai'. These chapters, then, do not only open up new national contexts for further evaluation but also offer dynamic case studies which demonstrate how national deployments of the medieval crusading past are formed out of modern experience, commemoration, and international competition, and how they have to be embodied in order to be enacted. In its combination of exploring new contexts of the use of the crusades and showcasing methodological variety the volume makes a distinctive contribution to our understanding of crusader medievalism and of nationalist uses of the past.

'Thinking with the nation': nations, national identity, and collective memories of the medieval past[15]

There is a vast literature on nations, national identity, and nationalism as well as libraries-worth of works written employing nationalist lenses or on national studies.[16] Building on theorists of nations and nationalism, and those of collective memory, this section will outline an understanding of nations (and so analysis of national identities) as contingent yet effective entities which can, and have, framed historical study and perceptions of the past. This will set the stage for the following section which will discuss the relationship between the crusades, crusading, and modern nations in order to provide an overview of ways in which the crusades have been studied and appropriated through national lenses.

Nationalism and national identity imply a nation, or at least an idea of a nation; nations, in Benedict Anderson's famous formulation, are 'an imagined political community'. They are *imagined* as a shared idea of a *community* of 'deep horizontal comradeship', *limited* with 'finite, if elastic boundaries', and *sovereign* in their ability to govern themselves as discrete political units.[17] Where a 'primordialist' view of nations understands them as reflections of an immutable collective national identity, a 'constructivist' position emphasises their created features and circumstances of production.[18] For theorist Ernest Gellner, 'Nations as a natural, God-given way of classifying men are a myth'.[19]

In his famous lecture at the Sorbonne in 1882 titled 'What is a Nation?' Ernest Renan observed that a nation 'presupposes a past'.[20] Nations represent an asserted continuity traced through history – the continuous existence of an entity (however constituted) back to an originary moment or embodiment. This is a re-narration of the past; a re-casting of events around and through the coherence brought by the modern nation. Nations, then, are themselves *narrations*: 'The stories we tell each other about our national belonging and being constitute the nation. These stories change over time and place and are always contested, often violently so.'[21] Observed by Homi K. Bhabha and Edward Said, the idea of nation-as-narration crystallises several features of the relationship between nations and history, not least the selective nature of national history writing. Indeed, for Renan, 'Forgetting, I would even go so far as to say historical error, is a crucial factor in the creation of a nation'.[22] As such, this national narration requires constant articulation and even recapitulation in the light of an evolving present: Renan called this contingent nature 'a daily plebiscite'.[23] Nations-as-narrations are always being formed and performed. For Bhabha, a nation's history 'may be half-made because it is in the process of being made; and the image of cultural authority may be ambivalent because it is caught, uncertainly, in the act of "composing" its powerful image.'[24] Indeed, its power may even come from its narrativity, as Peter Mandler has suggested.[25]

Lest the discussion above leave the impression of nations and national histories as all-powerful, monolithic generators of identity and perspective, their plastic nature renders nations perpetual *negotiations*; their status at any given point is the negotiated result of internal and external competition. Like Maurice Halbwachs' conception of collective memory a national identity has to be embodied; the nation needs to be expressed and performed to be made meaningful.[26] As a consequence of this necessary embodiment, national identity is also subject to the heterodox and contradictory beliefs held simultaneously by individuals and by groups. National identities may sit more or less comfortably with regional or transnational identities, or even other national identities within individuals or group. Moreover, if 'national consciousness' precedes nations by imagining a not-yet-existent nation with the hope of calling it into being, as E.J. Hobsbawm argued, then contemporary nations potentially bear within themselves protonational communities.[27] The result is a collective identity which is unevenly distributed, potentially incoherent and subject to change over time. This does not have to render a national identity less potent, especially when allied to dominant institutions or communities.

The limits of the nation: international histories, transnational dimensions

A national analysis of crusading memory takes seriously the presentist nature of nations, and the power of the idea (or versions of it) to shape perceptions of the past through its embodiment in people, places, and practices. Theorists and historians alike have warned of the danger of any historical analysis which centres nations taking nations at face-value, and so reproducing the forces which created and now sustain them. By 'forces' I mean the embodied interests and institutions which have shaped not only what individual nations are like but also the very idea of a nation itself. This 'methodological nationalism':

> references 'a perspective that equates society with national society', obscures any lived reality beyond a national conceptual frame, and 'gains its position as the natural way of looking at the

world from the fact that it 'adopts categories of practice as categories of analysis'.[28]

Theorists of collective memory have recognised the gravity national perspectives exert, exemplified by the work of Pierre Nora on French memory which precipitated a boom for memory studies.[29] More recently, and in reaction, Astrid Erll has coined the term 'travelling memory' to suggest that memories must be 'remediated' to function: they only become meaningful when communicated or transposed from one context to another.[30] If national history writing 'freezes' persons or events, fixing their meaning in relation to other events in order to present a continuity of national history or exemplar of national character, the very fixity this requires co-opts memory into something else, a *nationalised* history I suggest. Coined by Michael Rothberg, the idea of 'multidirectional memory' suggests that rather than seeing memories as 'zero sum' – either possessed by a group or not – memory is: 'subject to ongoing negotiation, cross-referencing, and borrowing; [it is understood] as productive and not privative.'[31] For our purposes here, this points to the ways in which memories of the crusades interact across national borders as well as flower within them. They exist within memory cultures which cultivate, prune, and regraft elements of those memories. Authors here seek to investigate those memories not as natural but as negotiated national narrations, asking *how* have national memories of the crusades developed? *Who* do they serve? And what happens when they cross national boundaries? These insights from memory studies serve to shift the focus to the transmission and polyvalent nature of collective memory, in contrast to nationalised memories.

The international nature of the crusades – which crossed borders, involved thousands of people from different 'national' communities, and do not fit easily into the history of a single modern nation – highlights the artificiality of rigidly applying national analysis to the memory (actually memories) of the crusades; 'Practically no crusade was truly national' wrote Richard.[32] This was true of the medieval crusading ventures, though it does not, of course, protect them from having been 'incongruously recruited to serve under national flags.'[33] Rather, it points us towards the transnational and international dimensions of crusader medievalism.

The crusading movement was more complicated than a set of glorious battles of the Franks or a proto-French colonial endeavour, for example, and cannot be reduced to the property of a single nation. Beyond nationalised histories, crusading has been used to stand for the united action of European 'Christendom' and even 'Western Civilisation' where the crusades have been interpreted as formational for a European identity or as one side in the enduring religio-cultural 'clash of civilisations'.[34] These crude appropriations subsume smaller national uses of the crusades but can, in turn, have localised national expressions. That General Francisco Franco's Nationalists promoted their cause in the Spanish Civil War (1936–39) – and his subsequent dictatorship – as a *cruzada* is a case in point. While the *cruzada* played as divine sanction for Franco's cause to a 'home' audience when promoted by the Spanish Catholic church, it simultaneously invited sympathy from Catholics worldwide, asking them to support the Nationalists as a local expression of an international conflict between 'godless communism' and Christianity.[35] These dimensions – national and transnational – illustrate the ability of crusading rhetoric and imagery to bring together local and global concerns and represent one of the tensions this volume explores.

Nations, the Middle Ages and the crusades

If, following the constructivist view, we understand nations as *narrations, negotiations*, and as *unnatural* entities, we can see how as ideas and identities they shape perceptions of the past. Given the medieval past's distance and traditional position as an 'other' to modernity, elements of the Middle Ages have repeatedly been appropriated for national ends.[36] This in turn has become an expected feature of national identity; so much so, for example, that Umberto Eco could label one of the presentist versions of the medieval past in his playful typology of medievalism as 'The Middle Ages of *national identities*'.[37] What do national identities – or those who construct or promote them – get from the medieval past? Often tangible ruins, legends, characters, documents, and events; the leaden 'stuff' which can be transmuted into so-called 'golden ages', origin myths and the continuing story of the nation.[38] These fragments form the elements which can be assembled into national mythistories, deployed by a range of actors to back-project national historical continuity and assert legitimacy in the present. The editors of *Whose Middle Ages?* wrote that 'origins help orient us [...] in the modern Western world, the Middle Ages serve as a gravitational point of history'.[39]

If theorists debate the applicability of national analyses to the pre-modern era – seeing nations as quintessentially modern and so any analysis of medieval national identity as anachronistic – there is no doubt that the medieval past has been (and still is) recruited and deployed in the service of modern national entities and interests.[40] And histories of both nations and nationalism often see the Middle Ages as generating the seeds of both. The rise of the modern nation-state as a political entity in the nineteenth-century was accompanied by the professionalisation of the historical discipline itself, within whose structures historians continue to operate.[41] National histories, and the 'nationalisation' of history in viewing the past through national lenses, were in Europe and beyond (often via imperial export) a product of the nineteenth-century:

> History was a crucial element with which to construct nations and national identity. Nation-builders everywhere agreed: their nation had to have a history – the longer and the prouder the better. Creating national historical consciousness was widely seen as the most important precondition for engendering true national feeling in the wider population, as both the ethnicization of the nation and its sacralisation only took shape against the background of history and heritage.[42]

Uses of the crusades, then, are a subset of broader relationship between nationalists and national histories which have repeatedly pressed the medieval past into the service of the present.

Given that nations and national identities in the present are invested in historical narratives, what does understanding nations and national identity in this way contribute to studies of the memories of the crusades? 'It cannot be denied that, under new guises, national feeling remains one of the mainsprings of the interest aroused by the history of the crusades' wrote Richard in 2005.[43] The crusades, as a prominent aspect of medieval European and Middle Eastern history, an expression of (Christian) sanctified warfare, and an arena of heroism, have offered a number of valuable avenues for those looking to the past for inspiration or authority.

National appropriations of crusading: historiographic overview

The first crusaders crossed Europe banded together in distinct contingents of shared language and loyalty to rival lords; later crusades were often organised, funded, and directed by monarchs whose participation came to define their course. Guibert of Nogent writing in (1108/21) argued that the First Crusade (1095–99) was the 'deeds of God through the Franks', reflecting what Susan Edgington has termed an 'incipient nationalism' in the historiography of the crusades.[44] Crusading offered England's King Richard I an international arena on which to project an image of his own bravery, chivalry, and valour – an opportunity he fully exploited before and after the Third Crusade. With the two expeditions of Saint Louis IX, king of France, in the thirteenth century (1248–54 and 1270), crusading became enduringly associated with the French. And while the military orders – birthed in the crusades – largely outlasted medieval crusading expeditions, they eventually succumbed to national appropriation. As even this skeleton outline illustrates, seeing the crusades through national (or proto-national) lenses encompasses groups defined by language, culture or monarchies and offers insight into the prosecution and later inscription of crusading.[45]

Scholarship on crusader medievalism has included both nation-bound studies following Elizabeth Siberry's meticulous work on uses of the crusades in Britain, and comparative works after Adam Knobler's pioneering and broad-ranging article.[46] Jonathan Phillips' *Holy Warriors* brought later twentieth and twenty-first century examples into dialogue with crusading history, while Christopher Tyerman's historiographical overview highlighted national traditions of scholarship and productions of manuscripts which became national projects.[47] More recently, chapters in volumes of *Engaging the Crusades* have highlighted national uses of the crusades – in German postcards of the First World War and in French postage stamps, for example.[48] The third volume in the series, edited by Felix Hinz and Johannes Meyer-Hamme, purposely sought out reflections from crusade historians from different national contexts. Summarising the contributions, Hinz and Meyer-Hamme noted that:

> In most cases – but by no means in all – the result of requesting the authors to write a characteristic story of the historical cultures of their respective country resulted in the authors employing the concept of the nation as an interpretative framework. The recourse to the concept of the nation served as a tool to facilitate classification.[49]

The responses reveal not only the variety of ways the crusades are framed today but also the ongoing utility of national analyses. So, contributions from Belgium and the UK emphasised national crusading heroes (Godfrey of Bouillon and King Richard I 'the Lionheart' of England), while German and Polish perspectives summoned the Teutonic knights. Views from Turkey, Syria, and Egypt asserted a continuity of Western aggression; a Russian response framed crusading

Introduction 11

as Western Christian expansionism, aimed at world domination, and thus operating on a continuum into the present through the Third Reich.[50] Emphasising local events within the history of the crusades, the Greek and Maltese sections referred to the Fourth Crusade and the Hospitaller Knights, respectively. We can see in microcosm here elements employed in national memories – heroes, events, and continuing identities (often the military orders).

Detailed work has been undertaken on French and British uses of the crusades. Historiographical studies have shown the initial interest in the crusades in French and German historical investigation in the nineteenth century shifting to Anglophone nations in the twentieth.[51] Before and during the First World War, crusading was entangled with British and French imperial intervention in the Mediterranean and Middle East, and it continued to have imaginative interest through the twentieth century in both countries.[52] The League of Nations' Mandates of Syria for France and Palestine for Britain – partly justified by historic connections with the Levant – heightened imaginative resonance for both nations: the French bought the Templar castle of Crac des Chevaliers in 1934 while the British eulogised General Allenby's 1917 capture of Jerusalem as the fulfilment of 'the Last Crusade'.[53] While there is room for more work to be done on British and French uses of the crusades the world beyond remains underserved, especially where Western European concepts of nationhood fit collective memories of the crusades less well or stifle productive new ways of thinking about how the crusades have been perceived and employed.[54]

Conclusion: national expressions, international import

An infamous internet meme depicts former US president Donald Trump dressed as a crusader knight in a Middle Eastern setting, riding on horseback holding a large American flag and under the direction and benediction of Pepe the frog dressed as the pope.[55] The image, popular among the far-right during Trump's presidency, encapsulates both the portability and the potency of crusading imagery. Here linked to American national imagery (the flag) it serves to evoke the idea of an ongoing 'clash of civilisations' between East and West, Muslims and Christians, and to promote the idea of Trump as an embodiment and champion of the enduring cause of the crusaders. Regardless of accuracy, the meme functions through simplification and quick association: here Trump as true America is linked to a militant, white, Christian, imperialist vision of past and present. Nationalised crusader medievalism remains potent and able to adapt to modern forms.

Using national lenses to view crusader medievalism, as this volume does, harnesses a powerful interpretative force to reveal contours of historical and contemporary appropriations of the crusades, crusaders, and crusading. There is of course a circularity here – looking for national pasts to emphasise the utility of national lenses tends to deliver nationalised histories (the 'methodological nationalism' mentioned above). Instead of stopping there, the understanding of nations outlined above allows us to perceive the presentist nature of nations and nationalised histories of the crusades and crusading. That is to say that nations and national identities exert gravity on the ways that the history of the crusades has been, and continues to be, written and received. Nations may be constructed, but their power comes from belief in their reality and the structuring of the world this entails. The interplay of nationalism, national identity and national historiographies, then, have generated histories and historical myths which have shaped the modern world. Perceptions of the past are, as I have said elsewhere, plastic but powerful, and nationalised images continue to exert considerable influence.[56]

In addition to moving the focus from Britain and France, generating new case studies and opportunities for greater comparative work, contributors' methodological variety demonstrates ways in which collective memory can 'travel' and can be 'multidirectional'. This volume reveals the constructed nature of uses of the crusading past in new contexts, and models ways of bringing together insights from studies in nationalism, memory, and medievalism.

Notes

1 Glyn W. Philpot, 'Richard I Leaving England for the Crusades, 1189', *ArtUK*, Parliamentary Art Collection, WOA 2601, 1925–27, <https://artuk.org/discover/artworks/richard-i-leaving-england-for-the-crusades-1189-214120>, [accessed 8 March 2022].
2 'The Building of Britain', *The Times,* 29 June 1927, p. 9.
3 Henry John Newbolt, *The Building of Britain* (London, 1927), p. 8; G.M. Trevelyan, *The History of England* (London, 1926), p. 163.
4 'The Building of Britain', *The Times,* 29 June 1927, p. 9. See Newbolt, *Building of Britain.*
5 'The Crusades Rooms', *Château de Versailles,* <https://en.chateauversailles.fr/discover/estate/palace/crusades-rooms#a-political-intent>, [accessed 26 January 2022].
6 Jean Richard, 'National Feeling and the Legacy of the Crusades', in *Palgrave Advances in the Crusades*, ed. Helen J. Nicholson (Basingstoke, 2005), p. 211.
7 Ibid, pp. 210–13.

8 Thomas Maissen, 'Introductory Remarks', in *National History and New Nationalism in the Twenty-First Century*, eds. Niels F. May and Thomas Maissen (Abingdon, 2021), p. 1.
9 Daniel Wollenberg, 'The New Knighthood: Terrorism and the Medieval', *Postmedieval* 5 (2014), pp. 21–33.
10 Andrew B.R. Elliott, *Medievalism, Politics and Mass Media* (Woodbridge, 2017); Nicholas L. Paul, 'Modern Intolerance and the Medieval Crusades', in *Whose Middle Ages?* eds. Andrew Albin et al. (New York, 2019), pp. 34–43.
11 See Francesca Petrizzo, '"Bad Crusader": Bohemond, the Scholars, and the Christchurch Shooter', in *The Crusades and the Far-Right: Engaging the Crusades, Volume Nine*, eds. Charlotte Gauthier and Jonathan Phillips (Abingdon, forthcoming).
12 See Sal Hagen, '"Deus Vult!": Tracing the Many (Mis)Uses of a Meme', *Open Intelligence Lab* (blog), 25 March 2018, <https://web.archive.org/web/20190629103451/https://oilab.eu/deus-vult-tracing-the-many-misuses-of-a-meme/>, [accessed 29 June 2019]; Adam Bishop, '#DeusVult', in *Whose Middle Ages?* pp. 256–64; Rory MacLellan, 'Far-Right Appropriations of the Medieval Military Orders', *The Mediæval Journal* 9 (2019), pp. 175–98; Gauthier and Phillips, eds., *The Crusades and the Far-Right*.
13 See Wollenberg, 'New Knighthood'; Elliott, *Medievalism*, p. 167; Paul, 'Modern Intolerance'; Paulo Pachá, 'Why the Brazilian Far Right Loves the European Middle Ages', *Pacific Standard*, 12 March 2019, https://web.archive.org/save/https://psmag.com/ideas/why-the-brazilian-far-right-is-obsessed-with-the-crusades, [accessed 13 May 2019]; 'Chapter 1 – The Cross and the Sword | Brazil – The Last Crusade', *Brasil Paralelo*, <https://www.youtube.com/watch?v=TkOlAKE7xqY&ab_channel=BrasilParalelo>, [accessed 21 January 2022] (with thanks to Pachá for this reference). For far-right uses of the past and of the crusades, see respectively: Louie Dean Valencia-García, ed., *Far-Right Revisionism and the End of History* (Abingdon, 2020); Gauthier and Phillips, eds., *The Crusades and the Far-Right*.
14 Akil N. Awan, 'Weaponising the Crusades: Justifying Terrorism and Political Violence', in *Engaging the Crusades, Vol. 2*, eds. Horswell and Awan, pp. 4–24; Jason T. Roche, '"Crusaders" and the Islamic State Apocalypse', *International Journal of Military History and Historiography* (2021), pp. 308–42.
15 For the title, see David Edgerton's blog, <https://www.davidedgerton.org/blog/2022/1/24/thinking-with-the-nation>, [accessed 3 February 2022].
16 E.g., see the literature referenced in John Breuilly, ed., *The Oxford Handbook of the History of Nationalism* (Oxford, 2013); Paul Lawrence, *Nationalism: History and Theory* (London: Routledge, 2014).
17 Benedict Anderson, *Imagined Communities*, 2nd revised edn. (London, 2016), pp. 6–7.
18 Adeed Dawisha, 'Nation and Nationalism: Historical Antecedents to Contemporary Debates', *International Studies Review* 4 (2002), pp. 3–22.
19 Quoted by Dawisha at ibid., p. 6., from Ernest Gellner, *Nations and Nationalism* (New York, 1983), p. 48.

20 Ernest Renan, 'What Is a Nation?', in *Nation and Narration*, ed. Homi K. Bhabha, trans. Martin Thom (Abingdon, 1990), p. 19.
21 Stefan Berger, 'Narrating the Nation: Historiography and Other Genres', in *Narrating the Nation*, eds. Stefan Berger, Linas Eriksonas, and Andrew Mycock (Oxford, 2008), p. 1.
22 Renan, 'What Is a Nation?', p. 11.
23 Ibid., p. 19.
24 Homi K. Bhabha, 'Introduction: Narrating the Nation', in *Nation and Narration*, ed. Bhabha, p. 3.
25 Peter Mandler, 'What Is "National Identity"? Definitions and Applications in Modern British Historiography', *Modern Intellectual History* 3 (2006), p. 280.
26 From the perspective of collective memory, see Maurice Halbwachs, *On Collective Memory*, ed. and trans. Lewis A. Coser (London, 1992), p. 188; Paul Connerton, *How Societies Remember* (Cambridge, 1989).
27 E.J. Hobsbawm, *Nations and Nationalism since 1780*, 2nd edn. (Cambridge, 1992), p. 11.
28 Glenda Sluga in Cemil Aydin et al., 'Rethinking Nationalism', *The American Historical Review* 127 (2022) p. 365.
29 For a summary article, see Pierre Nora, 'Between Memory and History: Les Lieux de Mémoire', trans. Marc Roudebush, *Representations* 26 (1989), pp. 7–24.
30 Astrid Erll, 'Travelling Memory', *Parallax* 17 (2011), pp. 4–18.
31 Michael Rothberg, *Multidirectional Memory* (Stanford, CA, 2009), p. 3.
32 Richard, 'Legacy of the Crusades', p. 206.
33 Tyerman, *Debate*, p. 4.
34 Tomaž Mastnak, 'Europe and the Muslims: The Permanent Crusade?', in *The New Crusades*, eds. Emran Qureshi and Michael A. Sells (New York, 2003), pp. 205–48; Geraldine Heng, 'Holy War Redux: The Crusades, Futures of the Past, and Strategic Logic in the "Clash" of Religions', *PMLA* 126 (2011), pp. 422–31; Kurt Villads Jensen, 'Cultural Encounters and Clash of Civilisations: Huntington and Modern Crusading Studies', in *Cultural Encounters During the Crusades*, eds. Kurt Villads Jensen, Kirsi Salonen, and Helle Vogt (Odense, 2013), pp. 15–26.
35 Mary Vincent, 'The Martyrs and the Saints: Masculinity and the Construction of the Francoist Crusade', *History Workshop Journal* 47 (Spring 1999), pp. 68–98; James Fountain, 'The Notion of Crusade in British and American Literary Responses to the Spanish Civil War', *Journal of Transatlantic Studies* 7 (2009), pp. 133–47; Ben Edwards, *With God on Our Side* (Newcastle upon Tyne, 2013).
36 See chapters on 'Middle', 'Modernity' and 'Presentism' in Elizabeth Emery and Richard Utz, eds., *Medievalism: Key Critical Terms* (Cambridge, 2014).
37 Umberto Eco, 'Dreaming of the Middle Ages', in *Travels in Hyperreality*, trans. William Weaver (London, 1987), p. 70.
38 See Patrick J. Geary, *The Myth of Nations* (Princeton, NJ, 2003); Anne-Françoise Le Lostec and Richard Utz, 'Moyen Âge et Nationalisme', in *Fake Moyen Âge! Ou Comment Le Moyen Âge Est Imaginé à Travers Les Films, La Bande Dessinée, Les Jeux Vidéo, La Pop Culture*, ed. Lauren Gerverau (Argentat-sur-Dordogne, Fr.: Nuage Vert, forthcoming), pp. 245–61.
39 Andrew Albin et al., eds., *Whose Middle Ages?* p. 90.

40 For the applicability of national analyses to the medieval past, see essays in Simon Forde, Lesley Johnson, and Alan V. Murray, eds., *Concepts of National Identity in the Middle Ages* (Leeds, 1995).
41 Paul Lawrence, 'Nationalism and Historical Writing', in *The Oxford Handbook of the History of Nationalism*, ed. John Breuilly (Oxford, 2013), p. 716.
42 Stefan Berger, 'Introduction: Towards a Global History of National Historiographies', in *Writing the Nation*, ed. Stefan Berger (Basingstoke, 2007), p. 1.
43 Richard, 'Legacy of the Crusades', p. 219.
44 Susan B. Edgington, 'The First Crusade: Reviewing the Evidence', in *The First Crusade*, ed. Jonathan Phillips (Manchester, 1997), p. 60. On national identity in the crusades and their chronicles, see Alan V. Murray, 'Questions of Nationality in the First Crusade', *Medieval History* 1 (1991), pp. 61–73; Marcus Bull, 'Overlapping and Competing Identities in the Frankish First Crusade', in *Le Concile de Clermont de 1095 et l'appel à Las Croisade* (Rome, 1997), pp. 195–211.
45 Tyerman, *Debate*, p. 4.
46 Siberry, *New Crusaders*; Elizabeth Siberry, *Tales of the Crusaders – Remembering the Crusades in Britain: Engaging the Crusades, Volume Six* (Abingdon, 2021); Horswell, *British Crusader Medievalism*; Knobler, 'Holy Wars'.
47 Jonathan Phillips, *Holy Warriors* (London, 2010), pp. 312–55; Tyerman, *Debate*.
48 Felix Hinz, '"May God Punish England!": Pseudo-Crusading Language and Holy War Motifs in Postcards of the First World War', in *Engaging the Crusades, Vol. 1*, eds. Horswell and Phillips, pp. 48–78; chapters by Rachael Pymm (pp. 91–110), and Tiago João Queimada e Silva (pp. 57–74), in *Engaging the Crusades, Vol. 2*, eds. Horswell and Awan; Elizabeth Siberry, 'Saint Louis: A Crusader King and Hero for Victorian and First World War Britain and Ireland', in *The Making of Crusading Heroes and Villains: Engaging the Crusades, Volume Four*, eds. Mike Horswell and Kristin Skottki (Abingdon, 2020), pp. 95–111; Felix Hinz and Johannes Meyer-Hamme, eds., *Controversial Histories – Current Views on the Crusades: Engaging the Crusades, Volume Three* (Abingdon, 2020).
49 Hinz and Meyer-Hamme, *Controversial Histories*, pp. 7–8.
50 Ibid., pp. 26–27.
51 Tyerman, *Debate*.
52 See Horswell, *British Crusader Medievalism*.
53 Astrid Swenson, 'Crusader Heritages and Imperial Preservation', *Past and Present* 226 (2015), p. 26; Horswell, *British Crusader Medievalism*, pp. 124–31.
54 For examples of broader work, see Matthias Determann, 'The Crusades in Arab School Textbooks', *Islam and Christian-Muslim Relations* 19 (2008), pp. 199–214; Matthew Gabriele, 'Debating the "Crusade" in Contemporary America', *The Mediaeval Journal* 6 (2016), pp. 73–92; Carsten Selch Jensen, 'Appropriating History: Remembering the Crusades in Latvia and Estonia', in *Remembering the Crusades and Crusading*, ed. Megan Cassidy-Welch (Abingdon, 2017), pp. 231–46; Simon John,

'A Crusader Duel at the Crystal Palace: The Statues of Godfrey of Bouillon and Richard the Lionheart at the Great Exhibition', *Journal of Victorian Culture* 20 (2021), pp. 1–19.; chapters by Sven Ekdahl, Eleni Sakellariou and Helen J. Nicholson in Helen J. Nicholson, ed., *Palgrave Advances in the Crusades* (Basingstoke, 2005).
55 See 'God Emperor Trump', *DeviantArt*, 13 July 2017, <https://web.archive.org/web/20220509163058/https://www.deviantart.com/generaltate/art/God-Emperor-Trump-692162369>, [accessed 9 May 2022]; Azeezah Kanji and Ivan Kalmar, 'Trump the "White Power Crusader" Defends Christianity Against a Jewish-Muslim Plot', *Haaretz*, 15 November 2018, <https://www.haaretz.com/us-news/.premium-trump-feeds-global-conspiracy-theories-of-a-jewish-muslim-plot-against-christianity-1.6654389>, [accessed 4 April 2022].
56 Mike Horswell, 'Deus Vult? Crusade Apologists, Historians and "Abortive Rituals" in the 1999 Reconciliation Walk to Jerusalem', *Práticas Da História* 9 (2019), p. 53.

Bibliography

Albin, Andrew, Mary C. Erler, Thomas O'Donnell, Nicholas L. Paul, and Nina Rowe, eds. *Whose Middle Ages?: Teachable Moments for an Ill-Used Past*. New York: Fordham University Press, 2019.

Anderson, Benedict. *Imagined Communities: Reflections on the Origin and Spread of Nationalism*. 2nd revised edn. London: Verso, 2016.

Awan, Akil N. 'Weaponising the Crusades: Justifying Terrorism and Political Violence'. In *The Crusades in the Modern World: Engaging the Crusades, Volume Two*. Eds. Mike Horswell and Akil N. Awan, 4–24. Abingdon: Routledge, 2020.

Aydin Cemil, Grace Ballor, Sebastian Conrad, Frederick Cooper, Nicole CuUnjieng Aboitiz, Richard Drayton, Michael Goebel, Pieter M Judson, Sandrine Kott, Nicola Miller, Aviel Roshwald, Glenda Sluga, and Lydia Walker, 'Rethinking Nationalism', *The American Historical Review* 127 (2022), pp. 311–71.

Berger, Stefan. 'Introduction: Towards a Global History of National Historiographies'. In *Writing the Nation: A Global Perspective*. Ed. Stefan Berger. Basingstoke: Palgrave Macmillan, 2007, pp. 1–29.

———. 'Narrating the Nation: Historiography and Other Genres'. In *Narrating the Nation: Representations in History, Media and the Arts*. Eds. Stefan Berger, Linas Eriksonas, and Andrew Mycock. Oxford: Berghahn Books, 2008, pp. 1–18.

Bhabha, Homi K. 'Introduction: Narrating the Nation'. In *Nation and Narration*. Ed. Homi K. Bhabha. Abingdon: Routledge, 1990, pp. 1–7.

Bishop, Adam. '#DeusVult'. In *Whose Middle Ages?: Teachable Moments for an Ill-Used Past*. Eds. Andrew Albin, Mary C. Erler, Thomas O'Donnell, Nicholas L. Paul, and Nina Rowe. New York: Fordham University Press, 2019, pp. 256–64.

Breuilly, John, ed. *The Oxford Handbook of the History of Nationalism*. Oxford: OUP, 2013.
Bull, Marcus. 'Overlapping and Competing Identities in the Frankish First Crusade'. In *Le Concile de Clermont de 1095 et l'appel à Las Croisade: Actes de Colloque Universitaire International de Clermont-Ferrand, 23–25 Juin 1995*. Rome: Collection de 'École Française de Rome, 1997, pp. 195–211.
'Chapter 1 – The Cross and the Sword | Brazil – The Last Crusade'. *Brasil Paralelo*. https://www.youtube.com/watch?v=TkOlAKE7xqY&ab_channel=BrasilParalelo. Accessed 21 January 2022.
'Crusades Rooms, The'. *Château de Versailles*. https://en.chateauversailles.fr/discover/estate/palace/crusades-rooms#a-political-intent. Accessed 26 January 2022.
Connerton, Paul. *How Societies Remember*. Cambridge: CUP, 1989.
Dawisha, Adeed. 'Nation and Nationalism: Historical Antecedents to Contemporary Debates'. *International Studies Review* 4 (2002), pp. 3–22.
Determann, Matthias. 'The Crusades in Arab School Textbooks'. *Islam and Christian-Muslim Relations* 19 (2008), pp. 199–214.
Eco, Umberto. 'Dreaming of the Middle Ages'. In *Travels in Hyperreality*. Trans. William Weaver. London: Picador, 1987, pp. 61–72.
Edgington, Susan B. 'The First Crusade: Reviewing the Evidence'. In *The First Crusade: Origins and Impact*. Ed. Jonathan Phillips. Manchester: MUP, 1997, pp. 55–77.
Edwards, Ben. *With God on Our Side: British Christian Responses to the Spanish Civil War*. Newcastle upon Tyne: Cambridge Scholars Publishing, 2013.
Elliott, Andrew B.R. *Medievalism, Politics and Mass Media*. Woodbridge: Boydell and Brewer, 2017.
Emery, Elizabeth, and Richard Utz, eds. *Medievalism: Key Critical Terms*. Cambridge: D.S. Brewer, 2014.
Erll, Astrid. 'Travelling Memory'. *Parallax* 17 (2011), pp. 4–18.
Forde, Simon, Lesley Johnson, and Alan V. Murray, eds. *Concepts of National Identity in the Middle Ages*. Leeds: University of Leeds, 1995.
Fountain, James. 'The Notion of Crusade in British and American Literary Responses to the Spanish Civil War'. *Journal of Transatlantic Studies* 7 (2009), pp. 133–47.
Gabriele, Matthew. 'Debating the "Crusade" in Contemporary America'. *The Mediaeval Journal* 6 (2016), pp. 73–92.
Gauthier, Charlotte, and Jonathan Phillips, eds. *The Crusades and the Far-Right: Engaging the Crusades, Volume Nine*. Abingdon: Routledge, forthcoming.
Geary, Patrick J. *The Myth of Nations: The Medieval Origins of Europe*. Princeton, NJ: Princeton University Press, 2003.
Gellner, Ernest. *Nations and Nationalism*. New York: Cornell University Press, 1983.
Hagen, Sal. '"Deus Vult!": Tracing the Many (Mis)Uses of a Meme'. *Open Intelligence Lab* (blog), 25 March 2018. https://web.archive.org/web/20190629103451/https://oilab.eu/deus-vult-tracing-the-many-misuses-of-a-meme/. Accessed 29 June 2019.
Halbwachs, Maurice. *On Collective Memory*. Ed. and trans. Lewis A. Coser. London: University of Chicago Press, 1992.

Heng, Geraldine. 'Holy War Redux: The Crusades, Futures of the Past, and Strategic Logic in the "Clash" of Religions'. *PMLA* 126 (2011), pp. 422–31.

Hinz, Felix. '"May God Punish England!": Pseudo-Crusading Language and Holy War Motifs in Postcards of the First World War'. In *Perceptions of the Crusades from the Nineteenth to the Twenty-First Century: Engaging the Crusades, Volume One*. Eds. Mike Horswell and Jonathan Phillips. Abingdon: Routledge, 2018, pp. 48–78.

Hinz, Felix, and Johannes Meyer-Hamme, eds. *Controversial Histories – Current Views on the Crusades: Engaging the Crusades, Volume Three*. Abingdon: Routledge, 2020.

Hobsbawm, E.J. *Nations and Nationalism since 1780: Programme, Myth, Reality*. 2nd edn. Cambridge: CUP, 1992.

Horswell, Mike. 'Deus Vult? Crusade Apologists, Historians and "Abortive Rituals" in the 1999 Reconciliation Walk to Jerusalem'. *Práticas Da História* 9 (2019), pp. 20–58.

———. *The Rise and Fall of British Crusader Medievalism, c. 1825–1945*. Abingdon: Routledge, 2018.

Jensen, Carsten Selch. 'Appropriating History: Remembering the Crusades in Latvia and Estonia'. In *Remembering the Crusades and Crusading*. Ed. Megan Cassidy-Welch. Abingdon: Routledge, 2017, pp. 231–46.

Jensen, Kurt Villads. 'Cultural Encounters and Clash of Civilisations: Huntington and Modern Crusading Studies'. In *Cultural Encounters During the Crusades*. Eds. Kurt Villads Jensen, Kirsi Salonen, and Helle Vogt. Odense: University Press of Southern Denmark, 2013, pp. 15–26.

John, Simon. 'A Crusader Duel at the Crystal Palace: The Statues of Godfrey of Bouillon and Richard the Lionheart at the Great Exhibition'. *Journal of Victorian Culture* 20 (2021), pp. 1–19.

Kanji, Azeezah, and Ivan Kalmar. 'Trump the "White Power Crusader" Defends Christianity Against a Jewish-Muslim Plot'. *Haaretz*, 15 November 2018. https://www.haaretz.com/us-news/.premium-trump-feeds-global-conspiracy-theories-of-a-jewish-muslim-plot-against-christianity-1.6654389. Accessed 5 April 2022.

Knobler, Adam. 'Holy Wars, Empires, and the Portability of the Past: The Modern Uses of Medieval Crusades'. *Comparative Studies in Society and History* 48 (2006), pp. 293–325.

Lawrence, Paul. 'Nationalism and Historical Writing'. In *The Oxford Handbook of the History of Nationalism*. Ed. John Breuilly. Oxford: OUP, 2013, pp. 713–30.

———. *Nationalism: History and Theory*. London: Routledge, 2014.

Le Lostec, Anne-Françoise, and Richard Utz. 'Moyen Âge et Nationalisme'. In *Fake Moyen Âge! Ou Comment Le Moyen Âge Est Imaginé à Travers Les Films, La Bande Dessinée, Les Jeux Vidéo, La Pop Culture*. Ed. Lauren Gerverau. Argentat-sur-Dordogne, Fr.: Nuage Vert, 2022, pp. 245–61.

MacLellan, Rory. 'Far-Right Appropriations of the Medieval Military Orders'. *The Mediæval Journal* 9 (2019), pp. 175–98.

Maissen, Thomas. 'Introductory Remarks'. In *National History and New Nationalism in the Twenty-First Century*. Eds. Niels F. May and Thomas Maissen. Abingdon: Routledge, 2021, pp. 1–22.

Mandler, Peter. 'What Is "National Identity"? Definitions and Applications in Modern British Historiography'. *Modern Intellectual History* 3 (2006), pp. 271–97.

Mastnak, Tomaž. 'Europe and the Muslims: The Permanent Crusade?' In *The New Crusades: Constructing the Muslim Enemy*. Eds. Emran Qureshi and Michael A. Sells. New York: Columbia University Press, 2003, pp. 205–48.

Murray, Alan V. 'Questions of Nationality in the First Crusade'. *Medieval History* 1 (1991), pp. 61–73.

Newbolt, Henry John. *The Building of Britain: A Series of Historical Paintings in St. Stephen's Hall, Westminster*. London: T. Nelson, 1927.

Nicholson, Helen J., ed. *Palgrave Advances in the Crusades*. Basingstoke: Palgrave Macmillan, 2005.

Nora, Pierre. 'Between Memory and History: Les Lieux de Mémoire'. Trans. Marc Roudebush. *Representations* 26 (1989), pp. 7–24.

Pachá, Paulo. 'Why the Brazilian Far Right Loves the European Middle Ages'. *Pacific Standard*, 12 March 2019. https://web.archive.org/save/https://psmag.com/ideas/why-the-brazilian-far-right-is-obsessed-with-the-crusades. Accessed 13 May 2019.

Paul, Nicholas L. 'Modern Intolerance and the Medieval Crusades'. In *Whose Middle Ages?: Teachable Moments for an Ill-Used Past*. Eds. Andrew Albin, Mary C. Erler, Thomas O'Donnell, Nicholas L. Paul, and Nina Rowe. New York: Fordham University Press, 2019, pp. 34–43.

Petrizzo, Francesca. '"Bad Crusader": Bohemond, the Scholars, and the Christchurch Shooter'. In *The Crusades and the Far-Right: Engaging the Crusades, Volume Nine*. Eds. Charlotte Gauthier and Jonathan Phillips. Abingdon: Routledge, forthcoming.

Phillips, Jonathan. *Holy Warriors: A Modern History of the Crusades*. London: Vintage, 2010.

Philpot, Glyn W. 'Richard I Leaving England for the Crusades, 1189'. *ArtUK*. Parliamentary Art Collection. WOA 2601. 1925–27. https://artuk.org/discover/artworks/richard-i-leaving-england-for-the-crusades-1189-214120. Accessed 8 March 2022.

Pymm, Rachael. 'Philatelic Depictions of the Crusades'. In *The Crusades in the Modern World: Engaging the Crusades, Volume Two*. Eds. Mike Horswell and Akil N. Awan. Abingdon: Routledge, 2020, pp. 91–110.

Renan, Ernest. 'What Is a Nation?' In *Nation and Narration*. Ed. Homi K. Bhabha, trans. Martin Thom. Abingdon: Routledge, 1990, pp. 8–22.

Richard, Jean. 'National Feeling and the Legacy of the Crusades'. In *Palgrave Advances in the Crusades*. Ed. Helen J. Nicholson. Basingstoke: Palgrave Macmillan, 2005, pp. 204–22.

Roche, Jason T. '"Crusaders" and the Islamic State Apocalypse'. *International Journal of Military History and Historiography* 41 (2021), pp. 308–42.

Rothberg, Michael. *Multidirectional Memory: Remembering the Holocaust in the Age of Decolonization*. Stanford, CA: Stanford University Press, 2009.

Siberry, Elizabeth. *The New Crusaders: Images of the Crusades in the 19th and Early 20th Centuries*. Aldershot: Ashgate, 2000.

———. 'Saint Louis: A Crusader King and Hero for Victorian and First World War Britain and Ireland'. In *The Making of Crusading Heroes and Villains: Engaging the Crusades, Volume Four*. Ed. Mike Horswell and Kristin Skottki. Abingdon: Routledge, 2020, pp. 95–111.

———. *Tales of the Crusaders – Remembering the Crusades in Britain: Engaging the Crusades, Volume Six*. Abingdon: Routledge, 2021.

Silva, Tiago João Queimada e. 'The Reconquista Revisited: Mobilising Medieval Iberian History in Spain, Portugal and Beyond'. In *The Crusades in the Modern World: Engaging the Crusades, Volume Two*. Eds. Mike Horswell and Akil N. Awan. Abingdon: Routledge, 2020, pp. 57–74.

Swenson, Astrid. 'Crusader Heritages and Imperial Preservation'. *Past and Present* 226 (2015), sup. 10, pp. 27–56.

Trevelyan, G.M. *The History of England*. London: Longmans, Green and Co., 1926.

Tyerman, Christopher. *The Debate on the Crusades*. Manchester: MUP, 2011.

Valencia-García, Louie Dean, ed. *Far-Right Revisionism and the End of History: Alt/Histories*. Abingdon: Routledge, 2020.

Vincent, Mary. 'The Martyrs and the Saints: Masculinity and the Construction of the Francoist Crusade'. *History Workshop Journal* 47 (Spring 1999), pp. 68–98.

Wollenberg, Daniel. 'The New Knighthood: Terrorism and the Medieval'. *Postmedieval* 5 (2014), pp. 21–33.

1 'Heroes and Martyrs'?
National Memories and Foreign Crusaders in Portuguese Commemorations of the Eighth Centenary of the Conquest of Lisbon (1947)

Pedro Martins

Introduction: remembering the medieval past in Portugal

On 15 May 1947, the inaugural day of the 'Eighth Centenary of the Conquest of Lisbon from the Moors' as it was officially called, at a solemn session held at the Lisbon Hall, the famed writer, former minister, diplomat, and current president of the *Academia das Ciências de Lisboa* (Academy of Sciences of Lisbon) Júlio Dantas (1876–1962) gave a speech about the taking of the city in 1147 in the context of the Second Crusade (1147–1150). According to Dantas, the foreign crusaders that helped the Portuguese king Afonso Henriques (*c.* 1109–1185) in this endeavour had been 'heroes and martyrs' who, 'by the force of arms, in the name of the Cross that guided them, determined Lisbon's European, universal and glaringly imperial destiny'. In Dantas' words, Lisbon, 'a city that was reborn, not only to the Portuguese but to Christendom and the world, had to be conquered by people of all nations'.[1]

This affirmation demonstrates two of the aspects that the organisers of the centenary wanted to stress regarding the role of foreign crusaders in the siege of Lisbon: on the one hand, that these warriors had essentially been guided by religious motives; on the other hand, that their participation prefigurated the 'cosmopolitan' or 'universal' character of the city – and by extension, of Portugal – later demonstrated by its colonial exploits.

In this chapter, I will examine the ways the organisers of the commemorations of the Eighth Centenary of the Conquest of Lisbon (1947) depicted the role of foreign crusaders in that enterprise. Attending to factors such as the diplomatic ties, colonial policy, and the bases of social and ideological support of the Portuguese dictatorship known as the *Estado Novo* ('New State', 1933–1974), as well as the historiographical constraints of such a representation, it will be demonstrated that the depiction of foreign crusaders was highly ambivalent, as the regime struggled to offer a unique and sanitised view of an event that many authors deemed as controversial. To achieve this goal, a set of official sources (programmes, books, booklets, posters, and photographs issued by the Portuguese government) and those non-official but subjected to press censorship (newspaper articles) were studied, in order to understand how foreign crusaders were represented and which factors influenced these representations. While the first set offers a depiction of the regime's portrayal of the conquest of Lisbon, the second demonstrates the various hesitations regarding both the event and the way it was commemorated.

Historical commemorations in nineteenth- and twentieth-century Europe have been the subject of a significant and increasing scholarly interest in recent decades. Eric Hobsbawm and Terence Ranger's 1983 seminal work demonstrated how the creation of public ceremonies was a key innovation as part of the so-called process of the 'invention of tradition' promoted by political and cultural elites in several European countries especially since the 1870s.[2] Concerning the commemoration of the medieval past, many authors have examined the contrived ways certain figures and events of the Middle Ages were appropriated to serve national narratives and ideological purposes in public centenaries and other festivals.[3]

In the Portuguese context, however, the academic interest for the subject has been more recent and less impressive.[4] The poor scholarly attention devoted to the Eighth Centenary of the Conquest of Lisbon is especially surprising, considering that it has been considered one of the main historical commemorations of the *Estado Novo* and the one that closed its 'first cycle' of official commemorative activism.[5] In addition, the capture of Lisbon in 1147, as well as its main sources – namely *De expugnatione Lyxbonensi* ('On the Conquest of Lisbon') – has been the subject of important studies by medievalists of international renown such as Jonathan Phillips and Susan B. Edgington.[6] According to Phillips, the conquest of the city was one of the 'few successes' of the Second Crusade.[7] The scarcity of eyewitness sources, the debates on their authorship, and their highly biased character contributed to historiographical controversies on the circumstances and events during the siege, namely the premeditated character of the crusaders' intervention and their behaviour just before and after the city's surrender.[8] The event also inspired a novel by the Portuguese Nobel Prize winner José Saramago, precisely titled *The History of the Siege of Lisbon*.[9]

'Heroes and Martyrs'? 23

This chapter will not only bridge a gap regarding the uses of the medieval past in twentieth-century Portuguese politics but will also raise questions on the relation between historiography and official commemorations, namely those related to the history of the crusades.

Late nineteenth- to mid-twentieth century

Similarly to what was happening in other European countries in the same period, late nineteenth-century Portuguese political elites understood that commemorating the past could be an important element of national cohesion. Auguste Comte's programme of a 'civil religion', which included the celebration of humanity's 'great men and achievements', was adopted by monarchical and republican individuals and associations alike.[10] As such, figures and events considered to have contributed to the progress of Portugal as nation were the subject of important commemorations. The Middle Ages, regarded as the period of birth and consolidation of national independence, were no exception to this.

Among the most celebrated medieval individuals were political leaders, primarily the first Portuguese king Afonso Henriques. The seventh centenary of his death was commemorated in 1885, an event that was a prelude of the great centenaries held during the next decades.[11] In 1894, the fifth centenary of the birth of Henry the Navigator was the subject of elaborate staging in Henry's hometown of Porto. Military leaders such as the constable Nuno Álvares Pereira (1360–1431) were also deemed worthy of public celebration, and a national holiday was created in 1920 to commemorate the day in which the Portuguese armies, led by Pereira, defeated the Castilian king at the Battle of Aljubarrota (1385).[12] But it was not only royals and warriors who earned a place in Portugal's civic calendar of medieval figures: in 1895, the eighth centenary of the birth of Saint Anthony (1195–1231) was also celebrated in Lisbon.[13]

In addition to individuals, some events of the Portuguese Middle Ages were regarded as significant in the context of historical commemoration. Conquests and battles assumed the highest place: the conquest of Ceuta (1415), whose fifth centenary was celebrated in 1915, the taking of Lisbon, and the battles of Aljubarrota and Ourique (1139), which were annually commemorated from 1920 and 1926, respectively. Ironically, the most important commemoration of a medieval 'event' – the eighth centenary of the 'foundation of Portugal' – was constrained to 1940, so that it coincided with the third centenary of the 'restoration of independence' from Spanish rule (1580–1640).[14]

Despite the historiographical controversy that this choice involved, the so-called 'double centenary' of 1940 represented the apogee of historical commemorations during the *Estado Novo* and served as model for the centenary of 1947.

Most of these celebrations took place at locations deemed as historically significant. Medieval buildings played a prominent role, especially after the campaign of monumental restoration conducted by the *Estado Novo*'s *Direcção-Geral dos Edifícios e Monumentos Nacionais* (General Directorate for National Buildings and Monuments, or DGEMN), created in 1929.[15] Among the most-used monuments were churches, cathedrals (Lisbon, Porto, Coimbra, Braga, Évora), convents (Carmo), and monasteries (Alcobaça, Batalha), common burial places of medieval kings and nobles, as well as castles, notably those linked to the figure of Afonso Henriques (Guimarães and São Jorge, in Lisbon). In addition to the cities associated with Portuguese medieval history, these commemorations were also organised at sites where famous battles had allegedly taken place. Vila Chã de Ourique (in the province of Ribatejo) and Castro Verde (in the Alentejo), competed for the location of the Battle of Ourique, while the promontory of Sagres (in the Algarve) was unanimously regarded as Henry the Navigator's base for his maritime voyages and place of death and, as such, was a focal point in the commemorations of 1960.

During the Portuguese military dictatorship (1926–33) and the *Estado Novo*, the commemorations of the medieval past assumed particular traits in comparison with the ones organised during the constitutional monarchy (1834–1910) and the First Republic (1910–26). The first difference was the sheer number of events: from 1926 to 1937 at least, the battles of Ourique and Aljubarrota were commemorated annually, in addition to the multiple centenaries of medieval figures (1931 and 1960, respectively, the fifth centenary of the deaths of Nuno Álvares Pereira and Henry the Navigator), and events (1932, 1934, and 1946, the fifth centenary of the so-called 'discovery of the Azores', the passing of the Cape Bojador, and the 'discovery of Guinea', as well as the aforementioned ones of 1940 and 1947). But the Portuguese dictatorial regimes did not only invest in quantitative terms; according to the historian Maria Isabel João, political authorities sought more control of these celebratory acts in terms of the organisation, programmes, and public ceremonies.

Similarly to contemporary fascist regimes, the *Estado Novo*, supported by paramilitary and other political organisations, made wide use of mass mobilisation and patronised historical re-enactments – pageants, jousts, displays, recitals, plays, exhibitions (notably the 1940

Exposição do Mundo Português or Exhibition of the Portuguese World; see Fig. 1.1) – and important historiographical publications.[16] In addition, these commemorations were accompanied by the inauguration of several public works, as part of the image of 'material restoration' that the regime wanted to convey. Finally, its conservative and authoritarian leanings were deeply embedded in the commemorations, namely in the constant references to the alliance between the State and the Church and the Catholic character of the Portuguese nation, and in the more or less explicit analogies between medieval political leaders and the head of government António de Oliveira Salazar (1889–1970).

Figure 1.1 The beginning of the *Cortejo do Mundo Português* (Pageant of the Portuguese World) at the *Exposição do Mundo Português*, 1940.

Source: Photo by Estúdio Horácio Novais. Col. Estúdio Horácio Novais I FCG – Biblioteca de Arte e Arquivos (CFT164.1195).

The Eighth Centenary of the Conquest of Lisbon: context, organisation and programme

Held two years after the end of the Second World War, the Eighth Centenary of the Conquest of Lisbon was organised in a context of economic problems, political tensions, and social upheaval. Although Portugal had remained neutral during the war, its economy was deeply affected by the international context, with goods shortages affecting most of its population and rising inflation.[17] The post-war political climate, in its turn, seemed to weaken the *Estado Novo*. Inside the regime, those who called for renovation clashed with those who stood for the return to hardline principles of fascism. Political opposition strengthened and demanded elections, called for November 1945, six months after the end of the war. In the words of Salazar, these elections would be 'as free as those in free England'.[18] However, as those held before, they would be disputed in a context of political repression, with the newly formed coalition of opposition forces called *Movimento de Unidade Democrática* (Movement of Democratic Union, or MUD) giving up and appealing for abstention. Notwithstanding the victory of the regime's party, *União Nacional* (National Union), the signs of distress were clear. In October 1946 and April 1947, two military coups unsuccessfully sought to overthrow Salazar. Between April 1945 and July 1947, a wave of strikes and protests led by rural and industrial workers and university students, and largely supported by the recently reorganised and clandestine Portuguese Communist Party (PCP), swept the whole country, eliciting a violent response from security forces. Similarly to previous historical commemorations, the Eighth Centenary of the Conquest of Lisbon was then part of a political struggle to convey a sense of national cohesion in a period of international changes and internal turmoil. As the historian Ernesto Castro Leal affirmed, it was an 'answer of political-symbolic convergence' of the *Estado Novo* to all attempts to overthrow it.[19]

The centenary spoke to international, national, and local dimensions of Lisbon. As had happened in the double centenary of 1940, it served as pretext to present the city as the capital of the Portuguese colonial empire, in a time when the wave of decolonisation was just starting in South and South-eastern Asia and the Middle East. At the same time, the commemorations were an opportunity to show Lisbon's fresh infrastructure developments, mainly conducted under the guidance of Salazar's recently deceased Minister of Public Works, Duarte Pacheco (1900–43).[20]

As to the localised character of the centenary, its planning was made by the Lisbon Municipality, which nominated three commissions, readily confirmed by government decree, to organise the event. The mayor of Lisbon himself, Álvaro Salvação Barreto, presided over the executive commission, which included several notable figures of the Portuguese political, intellectual, and artistic milieu of the time. Similarly to what happened during the double centenary of 1940, political authorities wanted to unite in the executive commission individuals of disparate fields, in order to demonstrate the unifying nature of the commemoration and to appease eventual personal tensions among the regime's supporting elites.

The celebrations were naturally centred in Lisbon and lasted roughly five months, from 14 May to 25 October – the date in which the Portuguese king and the crusaders had entered the city. Although the city's siege had only started in late June, mid-May was chosen as the beginning of the commemorations so that they did not coincide with 13 May (the day of the first Marian apparitions in Fatima) but overlapped with Lisbon's most important annual event, the feasts of Saint Anthony on 13 June.[21]

The centenary included multiple events of religious, civic, military, cultural, and recreational character. It started on the evening of 14 May with the re-enactment of a medieval battle at the Castle of São Jorge, followed by the 'appearance of an illuminated cross' on the fortress's walls, accompanied by the ringing of bells in every city church and music performances across Lisbon's streets.[22] On the morning of the next day, the so-called 'sword of Afonso Henriques', kept at the Porto Military Museum, reached Lisbon, touring the country from north to south with stops in Coimbra and Santarém; a route that was meant to represent the expansion of the Portuguese frontiers during the reign of Afonso Henriques and his successful military campaigns against Muslim political powers. After the sword was ceremoniously received by the Minister of War at the São Jorge Castle, a *Te Deum* was sung in the Cathedral of Lisbon on the afternoon of the same day. This religious moment took place in the presence of the President of the Republic Óscar Carmona, Salazar, all members of the government, the mayors of Lisbon and Porto, other political dignitaries, the Cardinal-Patriarch of Lisbon, as well as descendants of the crusaders and Portuguese nobles that had participated in the city's siege. The first day closed with a solemn session at the Lisbon Town Hall, in which some members of the government, the mayor of Lisbon and the Cardinal-Patriarch also participated.[23]

28 *Pedro Martins*

Other notable events included in the commemorations were: a vigil of arms performed by the *Mocidade Portuguesa* (Portuguese Youth), the dictatorship's youth organisation, at the Castle of São Jorge (27 May); the *Cortejo dos Municípios* (Pageant of the Municipalities), with representations from all parts of Portugal (1 June); an evocation of city's chroniclers (3 June); an exhibition on the life of Saint Anthony in the cathedral (13–23 June); the *Grande Festa do Tejo* (Great Feast of the Tagus), a parade of vessels from several parts of the country (29 June); the *Grande Cortejo Histórico de Lisboa* (Great Historical Pageant of Lisbon), representing Lisbon's history from its Christian conquest to modern times (6 and 20 July); a cycle of conferences on the city's history (6–24 October); a bibliographical exhibition on the conquest of Lisbon, displayed at the National Library (inaugurated on 21 October); the inauguration of a statue of Afonso Henriques at the Castle of São Jorge (25 October); and a display of fireworks by the river Tagus, as the closing moment of the centenary (26 October). This abundance of events demonstrates the importance that the organisers conferred on the commemoration in an effort to make the most of the centenary's calendar.

According to Leal, the central government was the major financier of the commemorations. It paid almost a half (6,000,000 *escudos*) of the total expenses of the centenary (15,663,688 *escudos*) and loaned a substantial part (5,000,000 *escudos*) to the Lisbon municipality. Moreover, 8,356,000 *escudos* were spent in the *Cortejo Histórico de Lisboa* on decorations and lightning, which revealed the importance that the organisers wanted the visual aspects of the centenary to confer.[24]

The depiction of the crusaders during the commemorations

Contested is the best adjective to describe the way the crusaders' role in the siege was represented in the centenary of 1947. At first glance, the depiction of the crusaders is clearly positive. As stated by the historian José Mattoso, the conquest of Lisbon was celebrated from 'the point of view of the conquerors' and, as such, it was represented as an 'absolute beginning' that completely erased the city's Islamic past.[25] As a conservative regime ideologically and socially supported by the Catholic Church, the *Estado Novo* wanted to portray the crusaders as 'heroes and martyrs' who had given their lives to protect the Christian faith and vanquish Islam – their common enemy with the Portuguese of that time. Their help in the siege of Lisbon was, thus, naturally described as highly beneficial and welcome. Simultaneously, the crusaders' involvement was represented as something that foreshadowed two aspects of Portuguese history.

The first was Portugal's (and Lisbon's in particular) 'cosmopolitan' character, later materialised in its overseas expansion and empire. This is an idea that several historians had advanced at least since the nineteenth century. In his 1879 *História de Portugal*, the notable Portuguese author Joaquim Pedro de Oliveira Martins had described the siege of Lisbon as an 'international council [...], in which Europe baptized the recent one [the Portuguese nation] in the light of history'. In Martins' words, 'the cosmopolitan character of its future life, of its later political physiognomy, seems to have been imposed since early, when, on that Tagus pool, where two hundred ships crowned with the flags of so many European nations stood, the cord of the Flemish, Lothringian, German and English armies was laid down'.[26] During the centenary of 1947, this idea would be corroborated by the organisers and participants. In a text published in the booklet containing the centenary's official programme, Joseph van der Elst, the Belgian envoy to Lisbon at the time, affirmed that, with its conquest by the European crusaders and Portuguese troops, the city had become 'the advanced citadel of western civilization', from which fifteenth-century sailors would start to explore the unknown parts of the globe.[27]

The second aspect allegedly foreshadowed by the crusaders' participation in the conquest of Lisbon was Portugal's future diplomatic ties. This aspect gave way to more or less explicit analogies with the present international situation and Portugal's current external relations. In the aforementioned booklet, the writer Urbano Rodrigues, for instance, characterised the crusaders' nationalities in a different manner: while the Germans were described as 'ferocious, uneven, exigent', the English were represented as a 'people of spirit and sentiment similar to ours'. In the same volume, the British ambassador to Portugal, Sir Owen St Clair O'Malley, stated that the siege of Lisbon had been 'the first time in which Portuguese and English blood was shed, fighting against their common enemy back then. It was on that occasion that the bonds that unite our two peoples, and which resulted in the creation of the Anglo-Portuguese alliance two centuries later, were forged'. The French ambassador to Lisbon, Jean du Sault, stressed that, 'from early on, Portuguese and French blood was together shed on the battlefields', which could be 'the origin of the almost instinctive sympathy' that brought closer the French and

Portuguese until present times.[28] These comments are revealing of an international context in which Portugal, a member of the Allied forces during the First World War and an unevenly neutral state during the Second World War (ambiguous in its initial stage and pro-Allied in its later one), wanted to foster its diplomatic ties with the victorious countries, namely with the ones that exerted a special geostrategic and economic influence.

But it was not only the centenary's participants that forged these analogies. In an article published during the second week of commemorations in the newspaper *República*, traditionally linked to the old left-wing republican opposition to the dictatorship, the poet, journalist, and MUD-supporter Augusto Casimiro affirmed that the conquest of Lisbon represented 'the first cooperation of our people with foreign nations'.[29] This statement probably reveals the aspirations from Portuguese opponents of the regime that the end of the war and the pressure of Western democratic nations could bring a quick end to the *Estado Novo*.

Notwithstanding this rather positive assessment of the crusaders' role in the siege, a closer look on the sources demonstrates that it was also undervalued by the centenary's participants. First of all, the programme of the centenary did not include commemorative events on the days of the departure of the crusaders' fleet from Dartmouth (23 May, according to most authors[30]) or of their arrival in Porto and Lisbon (16 and 28 June respectively). This fault earned criticism from the journalist, novelist, and MUD-supporter Francisco da Rocha Martins, in an article dated from the centenary's inaugural day and published in *República*. According to Martins, the chosen day to start the commemorations in Lisbon (15 May) did not have any historical significance, having been merely chosen 'to make the most of the long and rainless summer days'.[31]

In the centenary's official speeches, the crusaders' participation in the conquest was also diminished to the benefit of the Portuguese. The protagonists were always the Portuguese troops and especially their king Afonso Henriques, identified as the 'rightful' Christian conquerors of the city, with the crusaders being depicted as mere 'helpers'. The introduction to a booklet issued by the Secretariat of National Information and Tourism (SNI), for instance, stated: 'On that audacious undertaking, the Portuguese were helped by crusader knights, who, sailing in 180 ships, were on route from Northern Europe to Palestine and, after a previous arrangement in Porto, docked by the Tagus to disembark their people and help the King of Portugal in his daring endeavour'.[32]

This subsidiary representation of the crusaders was also visible in the centenary's solemn events. In the already mentioned speech on the opening day of the commemorations, Dantas criticised those that considered the conquest of Lisbon 'more a foreign military endeavour than a national victory' and, as such, an event unworthy of commemoration. Calling the attention to the biased character of the available sources on the siege, Dantas emphasised that Afonso Henriques had already decided to conquer the city and that the Portuguese army, which was at least as powerful as the one of the crusaders, was already on the way to Lisbon even before their fleet arrived in Porto. According to Dantas, the Portuguese king had been the one that, during the siege, had 'ensured the unity of command of such disparate peoples', dominated the far-fetched ambitions of the greedier crusaders and ordered the construction of the second siege tower, which was proven to be decisive in the taking of the city. In Dantas' words, the Portuguese king was 'the man to whom we owe the glory of being free – and being who we are.'[33]

The bishop of Porto, Pedro Pitões, who exhorted the crusaders to help Afonso Henriques, also deserved a special appraisal. On the 17 June, near the city's cathedral, the Porto municipality inaugurated a memorial plaque that stated: 'On the 17th of June 1147, the bishop Pedro Pitões preached on this spot to the Nordic crusaders, exhorting them to help Afonso Henriques in the conquest of Lisbon from the Moors, a military endeavour in which he devotedly participated.' In a session later held in the *Sociedade de Geografia de Lisboa* (Lisbon Geographic Society), the president of the Municipality, Luís de Pina, delivered a speech in which he expressed his admiration for the bishop's oratorical skills and further support in the conquest of Lisbon. According to Pina, it was Pedro Pitões' power of persuasion that convinced the crusaders of the righteousness and holy character of their military endeavour, thus preventing them from sailing immediately to the Holy Land or later rebelling against the Portuguese king.[34]

The apparent rivalry between the representations of the Portuguese and those of the crusaders was especially visible in the way their attitudes towards the Muslim and Mozarabic population of Lisbon was depicted. While the Portuguese king and his troops were portrayed as benevolent, honoured, and civilised, foreign crusaders, in particular the Rhineland and Flemish ones, were, following the description of *De expugnatione Lyxbonensi*, essentially described as greedy, barbaric, and violent. Even those authors who did not participate in the commemorations followed this pattern of representation. For instance, in the aforementioned article, Augusto Casimiro praised 'the magnificent and human lesson of that king [Afonso Henriques] crowned by the rude and democratic people of the *concelhos*,[35] who imposes confidence on his adversaries – who fear, respect and trust him – and serenely corrects the barbarians' [i.e., the crusaders] abuses'. According to Casimiro, the value and meaning of the conquest of Lisbon far exceeded 'the barbaric mentality and turbulent greed of the foreigners'.[36]

Although also present in official publications, this dichotomy in the depiction of the conduct of Portuguese troops and foreign crusaders was not so stark, probably in order to not offend the diplomatic representations that participated in the centenary. In a text published in the booklet containing the centenary's official programme, the historian Gustavo de Matos Sequeira, for instance, affirmed that Afonso Henriques, his bishops and troops 'knew how to destroy the dissensions and medieval rudeness of the fiery Northern crusaders'. The tolerance of the Christian conquerors of Lisbon towards the city's inhabitants was also emphasised by Pietro Ciriaci, Apostolic Nuncio to Portugal, in an official salute published in the same volume. According to the prelate, this was a conduct that strongly contrasted with the one that led to post-war 'processes of population transfer' in Eastern Europe.[37] In a text published in the official book *Lisboa: oito séculos de História*, José Augusto de Oliveira, responsible for the 1935 translation of *De expugnatione Lyxbonensi* into Portuguese, in his turn claimed that the violence exerted by some crusaders against the population of Lisbon could only have lasted a few hours, because the other crusader soldiers would not permit that the city's spoils were not shared equally among all.[38]

In the centenary's visual representations, the crusaders' presence was recognised, even if in a rather subsidiary manner. At the *Cortejo Histórico de Lisboa*, for instance, the crusaders were portrayed by ten members of the French, English, Belgian, Dutch, and German communities of Lisbon, dressed in medieval garments. However, while the actor playing Afonso Henriques was riding a horse, the 'crusaders' were on foot, carrying a canopy that sheltered the Portuguese king (see Fig. 1.2). In the booklet containing the centenary's official programme, they were merely described as 'the crusaders that helped in the Conquest of Lisbon'.[39]

In the centenary's official iconography (posters, book covers, medals), the crusaders were either absent or appeared as background for the Portuguese king. In some cases, they are only implicitly represented by a sword and a cross – symbols also traditionally associated

Figure 1.2 'King Afonso Henriques' surrounded by the crusaders at the *Cortejo Histórico de Lisboa*, 6 July 1947.

Source: Photo by Estúdio Horácio Novais. Col. Estúdio Horácio Novais I FCG – Biblioteca de Arte e Arquivos (CFT164.22851).

with Afonso Henriques – often superimposing a crescent, symbol of Islam (Figs. 1.3–1.7). For instance, the centenary's commemorative medal, designed by the sculptor Álvaro de Brée (Fig. 1.8), represented, in the words of the historian Pedro Batalha Reis:

> the dominating figure of Afonso Henriques raising his sword, with the great shield similar to the one used by the crusaders who helped him in the conquest of the City […]. Completing the expressive symbolism of the meaning of that impressive medal, we have on the left tower the Cross, placed there by the warrior that had just overthrown the Muslim crescent from its last redoubt.[40]

It is thus noticeable how foreign crusaders did not play a significant role in the centenary's historical depictions. Instead, the active role in the defeat of the entity represented as the enemy – Islam – was attributed to the Portuguese king Afonso Henriques.

34 Pedro Martins

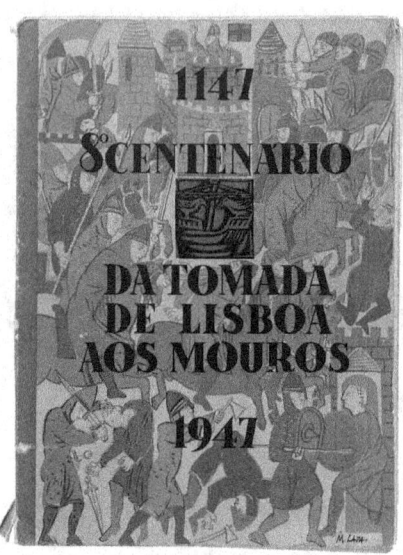

Figure 1.3 Cover of the booklet containing the official programme of the centenary, designed by Manuel Lapa.

Source: *Programa Oficial das Comemorações do VIII Centenário da Tomada de Lisboa* (Lisbon, 1947).

Figure 1.4 Cover of the children's book by Leyguarda Ferreira, *A conquista de Lisboa aos Mouros* (Lisboa: Romano Torres, 1947). Design by Litografia Amorim.

'Heroes and Martyrs'? 35

Figure 1.5 Official poster of the centenary.
Source: Torre do Tombo National Archive (PT/TT/SNI/CG/0005/0041).

Figure 1.6 Official poster of the centenary.
Source: Torre do Tombo National Archive (PT/TT/SNI/CG/0005/0040).

Figure 1.7 Official poster of the centenary.
Source: Torre do Tombo National Archive (PT/TT/SNI/CG/0005/0039).

Figure 1.8 Commemorative medal of the centenary, designed by the sculptor Álvaro de Brée.
Source: INCM/Museu Casa da Moeda 1737.

Conclusion

This chapter has examined the representation of foreign crusaders in the so-called 'Eighth Centenary of the Conquest of Lisbon from the Moors', commemorated in 1947. This is an event that can be inscribed in a long series of state-patronised historical commemorations organised at least since the late nineteenth century. Similarly to these celebrations, the Eighth Centenary of the Conquest of Lisbon was an important episode in Portuguese nation-building, attempting to forge a shared narrative about a historical event that today is still the subject of historiographical enquiry and debate. Regarded by nineteenth-century romantic and historicist culture as the epoch of origin of European nations, the Middle Ages played a relevant role in these nation-building processes, and Portugal was no exception to this. Medieval kings and warriors – in this case Afonso Henriques and the troops that conquered Lisbon in 1147 – emerged as national heroes, examples of virtues and values that should be preserved and cherished in the modern world.

The crusaders that participated in the endeavour were, however, represented with much more ambivalence during the centenary. On the one hand, they were depicted as valorous Christian knights and natural allies of the Portuguese people who delayed their journey to the Holy Land and gave their lives to liberate an Iberian city from Muslim dominion. This attitude not only allegedly proved the Christian and cosmopolitan character of the Portuguese nation, but also foreshadowed its future diplomatic ties with several northern and central European nations. On the other hand, the crusaders' military role and behaviour after the city's conquest remained a matter of some controversy. While the centenary's organisers sought to emphasise the martial skills and moral value of the Portuguese troops, and especially their leader Afonso Henriques, they were fully aware of the essential part played by the crusaders during the siege, notwithstanding some alleged abuses committed in its aftermath. The fact that the authorship of the most important sources on the conquest of Lisbon is commonly attributed to foreigners had some impact on these depictions, since it was used to raise suspicions of their partiality and to highlight the Portuguese participation.

Behind this ambivalent depiction of the crusaders lay factors of religious, political, diplomatic, nationalistic, and historiographical nature. First, as a Catholic-supported authoritarian regime, the *Estado Novo* sought to convey an image of the constitution of the Portuguese territory as a religiously motivated endeavour, part of a larger war against the enemies of the Christian faith. The association between the Second Crusade and the so-called Iberian *Reconquista*, and specifically the siege of Lisbon, provided the perfect context to convey this image.

Second, the longstanding historiographical tradition of depicting the foreign crusaders' endeavour as a proof of the nation's cosmopolitan character fitted well into the regime's colonial policy. After decades of German and British interest in the Portuguese possessions in Africa and in a time of emerging decolonisation, the *Estado Novo* wanted to affirm its role as guardian of the old Portuguese empire. The assumption that the Portuguese were a 'cosmopolitan people', with a special inclination to dialogue and mingle with other societies – which was later designated as *Luso-tropicalismo* ('luso-tropicalism') – served the international image that the regime wanted to disseminate during the following years.[41]

Third, the ways foreign crusaders were depicted in the centenary reflected Portugal's diplomatic stances towards several countries in post-war Europe. Most of the crusaders' nationalities, especially the Anglo-Normans, were depicted in a positive light, which, to some extent, contrasted with the representation of the Rhenish (or German) crusaders. This was a consequence of the special relationship that Portugal maintained with Britain, usually considered its oldest ally and main European diplomatic partner, and the rather indifferent or distant attitude towards Germany in the aftermath of its defeat in 1945. While Portuguese diplomatic relations with Germany were suspended from 1945 to 1951, the country kept strong ties with most Western European nations and would soon be a founding member of the OEEC (1948) and NATO (1949). Thus, the crusaders' participation in the siege was depicted as a prologue to Portugal's future political and military ties with other foreign powers.

Fourth, nationalism played a significant role in the crusaders' depictions. Regarded as an important step in the formation of the Portuguese territory, the conquest of Lisbon – both future capital of the emerging kingdom and head of a colonial empire – was represented as an essentially Portuguese endeavour, even if helped by foreigners. To depict it otherwise would be considered a cause of national embarrassment and would undermine Portugal's legitimacy as an independent nation – something that in a deeply nationalist regime such as the *Estado Novo* was regarded as intolerable.

Finally, it is important to mention that historiographical studies on the relationship between the medieval Portuguese kingdom and the crusades were, at the time, either incipient or poorly known in the national context. As Mattoso has affirmed, instead of financing research on the history of the conquest of Lisbon, at the time of the commemoration the Portuguese government concentrated its efforts on performative aspects and on monumental restoration, privileging an 'exhortative rhetoric centred on national virtues' and on the exploration of historiographical myths, in order to reinforce 'social and political cohesion'.[42] In addition, prolific scholars that had recently researched the relations between Portuguese medieval monarchs and the papacy or the origins of the idea of crusading in Portugal, such as Carl Erdmann, received poor public attention.[43] Questions about the siege of Lisbon, such as the authorship of the known sources, the premeditated character of the crusaders' intervention or their behaviour in the aftermath of the conquest remained in obscurity and instead served to feed national prejudices.

While in recent decades many medievalists have conducted research on these topics, it is interesting to note how the aforementioned nationalist rhetoric still pervades the Portuguese public space. In the recent 2021 presidential campaign, for instance, the right-wing populist candidate André Ventura used Portuguese medieval figures such as Afonso Henriques and invoked the need of a 'new *reconquista*'.[44] This not only echoes the primal importance of this king in Portuguese historical culture but also the pervasive view of the Middle Ages, and specifically the Iberian and Portuguese Middle Ages, as a period of profound antagonism between Christianity and Islam. Ventura's result in the presidential elections (third place, with 11.9% of votes) might be a good indicator of how commemorations such as the one of 1947 have left a profound impression on the popular perception of Portuguese medieval history.

Notes

1 Júlio Dantas, Speech at the solemn session held in the Lisbon Town Hall on the inaugural day of the 'Eighth Centenary of the Conquest of Lisbon from the Moors', *Revista Municipal. Ano Comemorativo do VIII Centenário da Tomada de Lisboa aos Mouros*, 2nd trimester 1947, p. 22.

2 Eric Hobsbawm, 'Mass-Producing Traditions: Europe, 1870–1914', in *The Invention of Tradition*, eds. Eric Hobsbawm and Terence Ranger (Cambridge, 1983), pp. 268–72.

3 On this subject, see for example Georges Duby, *The Legend of Bouvines* (Berkeley and Los Angeles, 1990), p. 174, on the seventh centenary of the Battle of Bouvines (1914); Elizabeth Emery and Laura Morowitz, *Consuming the Past* (Aldershot, 2003), pp. 24–25, on the commemorations of Jeanne d'Arc in late nineteenth- and early twentieth-century France; Stefan Schweizer, *'Unserer Weltanschauung sichtbaren Ausdruck geben': nationalsozialistische Geschichtsbilder in historischen Festzügen zum 'Tag der Deutschen Kunst'* (Göttingen, 2007), pp. 153–62, on the depiction of German medieval history at the pageant '1000 Years of German History' (1937); Tommaso di Carpegna Falconieri, '"Medieval" identities in Italy: national, regional, local', in *Manufacturing Middle Ages*, eds. Patrick Geary and Gábor Klaniczay (Leiden, 2013), pp. 337–38, on medievalised local festivals in late-nineteenth and early-twentieth century Italy.

4 Sérgio Campos Matos, 'O V Centenário Henriquino (1960): Portugal entre a Europa e o Império', in *O Fim da Segunda Guerra Mundial e os novos rumos da Europa*, ed. António José Telo (Lisbon, 1996), pp. 153–69; Fernando Rosas, 'O 14 de Agosto. As Aljubarrotas do Estado Novo', *História* 3 (1998), pp. 46–53; Maria Isabel João, *Memória e Império* (Lisbon, 2002); Ernesto Castro Leal, 'Poder e comemoração: Festa do Patriotismo, Festa da Pátria em Portugal (1920–1938)', *Turres Veteras* 8 (2006), pp. 275–83; Ernesto Castro Leal, 'Comemorações, poderes e espectáculo: o VIII Centenário da Tomada de Lisboa aos Mouros em 1947', in *I Colóquio Temático O Município de Lisboa e a Dinâmica Urbana (sécs. XVI–XX)* (Lisbon, 1998), pp. 473–96; Ernesto Castro Leal, 'Poder, Memória e Glória: comemoração do 8° centenário da tomada de Lisboa aos mouros', *Revista Portuguesa de História* 36 (2002–2003), pp. 313–34.
 5 Arlindo Manuel Caldeira, 'O poder e a memória nacional. Heróis e vilãos na mitologia salazarista', *Penélope* 15 (1995), p. 129; Ernesto Castro Leal, *Nação e Nacionalismos* (Lisbon, 1999), pp. 83–84.
 6 Jonathan Phillips, 'Ideas of Crusade and Holy War in De Expugnatione Lyxbonensi (The Conquest of Lisbon)', *Studies in Church History* 36 (2000), pp. 123–41; Susan B. Edgington, 'The Capture of Lisbon: Premeditated or Opportunistic?', in *The Second Crusade*, eds. Jason T. Roche and Janus Møller Jensen (Turnhout, 2015), pp. 257–72.
 7 Phillips, 'Ideas of Crusade', p. 123.
 8 Jonathan Phillips, 'St Bernard of Clairvaux, The Low Countries and the Lisbon Letter of the Second Crusade', *The Journal of Ecclesiastical History* 48 (1997), pp. 485–97; Jason T. Roche, 'The Second Crusade: Main Debates and New Horizons', in *The Second Crusade*, pp. 27–28; Edgington, 'Capture of Lisbon', pp. 257–72.
 9 José Saramago, *The History of the Siege of Lisbon*, trans. Giovanni Pontiero (London, 1996) [original Portuguese version: *História do cerco de Lisboa* (Lisbon, 1989)].
10 Leal, *Nação e Nacionalismos*, p. 50.
11 Sérgio Campos Matos, 'D. Afonso Henriques na cultura histórica oitocentista', in *2° Congresso Histórico de Guimarães*, vol. 3 (Guimarães, 1997), pp. 233–35.
12 Leal, 'Poder e comemoração', pp. 275–83.
13 António Ventura, 'A contestação ao Centenário Antoniano de 1895', *Lusitania Sacra* 8–9 (1996–97), pp. 361–83.
14 Luís Miguel Oliveira Andrade, *História e Memória. A Restauração de 1640: do Liberalismo às Comemorações Centenárias de 1940* (Coimbra, 2001), pp. 200–07.
15 Maria João Baptista Neto, *Memória, Propaganda e Poder* (Porto, 2001).
16 João, *Memória e Império*, p. 393.
17 Fernando Rosas, *Portugal entre a Paz e a Guerra, 1939–1945* (Lisbon, 1990), pp. 75 and 337–39.
18 António de Oliveira Salazar, 'Uma entrevista com o Presidente do Conselho', interview by António Ferro, *Diário de Notícias*, 14 November 1945, p. 5.
19 Leal, 'Poder, Memória e Glória', pp. 316–20.
20 Ibid., p. 315.

21 Ibid., p. 332.
22 *Programa Oficial das Comemorações do VIII Centenário da Tomada de Lisboa* (Lisbon, 1947).
23 *Diário de Notícias*, 16 May 1947, pp. 1 and 4.
24 Leal, 'Poder, Memória e Glória', p. 329.
25 Mattoso, 'No 850° aniversário da conquista de Lisboa', *Arqueologia Medieval* 7 (2001), p. 12.
26 Joaquim Pedro de Oliveira Martins, *Historia de Portugal*, vol. 1, 3rd edn. (Lisbon, 1882), pp. 83–84.
27 *Programa Oficial das Comemorações*.
28 Ibid.
29 Augusto Casimiro, 'Lições do passado', *República*, 24 May 1947, p. 1.
30 Charles Wendell David, ed., *De Expugnatione Lyxbonensi* (New York, 1936), p. 59; Edgington, 'The Capture of Lisbon', p. 267.
31 Francisco da Rocha Martins, 'Fastos e Festas', *República*, 14 May 1947, pp. 1 and 5.
32 *Festas do 8° Centenário da Tomada de Lisboa aos Moiros* (Lisbon, 1947), p. 1.
33 Júlio Dantas, Speech at the solemn session held in the Lisbon Town Hall on the inaugural day of the 'Eighth Centenary of the Conquest of Lisbon from the Moors', pp. 21–23.
34 Luís de Pina, 'O Porto na conquista de Lisboa', in *Duas cidades ao serviço de Portugal*, vol. 1 (Porto, 1947), pp. 30–37.
35 *Concelho*: Portuguese word for municipality.
36 Casimiro, 'Lições do passado', p. 1.
37 *Programa Oficial das Comemorações*.
38 José Augusto de Oliveira, 'A conquista de Lisboa', in *Lisboa: oito séculos de História*, ed. Gustavo de Matos Sequeira (Lisbon, 1947), pp. 139–40.
39 *Programa Oficial das Comemorações*.
40 Pedro Batalha Reis, *A Medalha Comemorativa do VIII Centenário da Conquista de Lisboa aos Mouros e o concurso que precedeu a sua escolha* (Lisbon, 1949), p. 10.
41 See Cláudia Castelo, *'O modo português de estar no mundo': O luso-tropicalismo e a ideologia colonial portuguesa (1933–1961)* (Lisbon, 1998).
42 Mattoso, 'No 850° aniversário da conquista de Lisboa', p. 11.
43 José Mattoso, 'Perspectivas actuais da investigação e da síntese na historiografia medieval portuguesa (1128–1383)', *Revista de História Económica e Social* 9 (1982), pp. 151–52. Though Erdmann's book on the relations between the papacy and twelfth-century Portuguese monarchs and his doctoral thesis on the idea of crusading in Portugal were recently translated to Portuguese language, his *habilitation* thesis on the origins of the idea of crusading in medieval Europe was not. Carl Erdmann, *O Papado e Portugal no primeiro século da história portuguesa* (Coimbra, 1935); *A idea de cruzada em Portugal* (Coimbra, 1940); *Die Entstehung des Kreuzzugsgedankens* (Stuttgart, 1935).
44 Hélder Gomes and José Fernandes, 'Como Ventura usou o imaginário nacionalista do Estado Novo e imitou Donald Trump', *Expresso*, 22 January 2021, <https://expresso.pt/presidenciais2021/2021-01-22-Como-Ventura-usou-o-imaginario-nacionalista-do-Estado-Novo-e-imitou-Donald-Trump>, [accessed 1 April 2022].

Bibliography

Primary

Casimiro, Augusto. 'Lições do passado'. *República*, 24 May 1947, p. 1.
Dantas, Júlio. Speech at the solemn session held in the Lisbon Town Hall on the inaugural day of the 'Eighth Centenary of the Conquest of Lisbon from the Moors', *Revista Municipal. Ano Comemorativo do VIII Centenário da Tomada de Lisboa aos Mouros*, 2nd trimester 1947, pp. 20–23.
Gomes, Hélder, and Fernandes, José. 'Como Ventura usou o imaginário nacionalista do Estado Novo e imitou Donald Trump'. *Expresso*. 22 January 2021. https://expresso.pt/presidenciais2021/2021-01-22-Como-Ventura-usou-o-imaginario-nacionalista-do-Estado-Novo-e-imitou-Donald-Trump. [Accessed 1 April 2022].
Martins, Francisco da Rocha. 'Fastos e Festas'. *República*, 14 May 1947, p. 1 and 5.
Martins, Joaquim Pedro de Oliveira. *História de Portugal*. Vol. 1. 3rd edn. Lisbon: Livraria Bertrand, 1882.
Oliveira, José Augusto de. 'A conquista de Lisboa'. In *Lisboa: oito séculos de História*. Ed. Gustavo de Matos Sequeira. Lisbon: Câmara Municipal de Lisboa, 1947, pp. 139–40.
Pina, Luís de. 'O Porto na conquista de Lisboa'. In *Duas cidades ao serviço de Portugal. Subsídios para o estudo das relações de Lisboa e Porto durante oito séculos*. Vol. 1. Porto: Câmara Municipal do Porto, 1947, pp. 30–37.
Programa Oficial das Comemorações do VIII Centenário da Tomada de Lisboa. Lisbon: Sociedade Astória, Lda., 1947.
Reis, Pedro Batalha. *A Medalha Comemorativa do VIII Centenário da Conquista de Lisboa aos Mouros e o concurso que precedeu a sua escolha*. Lisbon: Câmara Municipal de Lisboa, 1949.
Salazar, António de Oliveira. 'Uma entrevista com o Presidente do Conselho', interview by António Ferro. *Diário de Notícias*, 14 November 1945, pp. 1 and 5.
Saramago, José. *The History of the Siege of Lisbon*, trans. Giovanni Pontiero. London: Harvill Press, 1996 [original Portuguese version: *História do cerco de Lisboa* (Lisbon: Caminho, 1989)].
Secretariado Nacional de Informação. *Festas do 8° Centenário da Tomada de Lisboa aos Moiros*. Lisbon: Edições SNI, 1947.

Secondary

Andrade, Luís Miguel Oliveira. *História e Memória. A Restauração de 1640: do Liberalismo às Comemorações Centenárias de 1940*. Coimbra: Minerva, 2001.
Caldeira, Arlindo Manuel. 'O poder e a memória nacional. Heróis e vilãos na mitologia salazarista'. *Penélope* 15 (1995), pp. 121–42.
Carpegna Falconieri, Tommaso di. '"Medieval" Identities in Italy: National, Regional, Local'. In *Manufacturing Middle Ages. Entangled History of Medievalism in Nineteenth-Century Europe*. Eds. Patrick Geary and Gábor Klaniczay. Leiden: Brill, 2013, pp. 317–45.

Castelo, Cláudia. *'O modo português de estar no mundo': O luso-tropicalismo e a ideologia colonial portuguesa (1933–1961)*. Lisbon: Afrontamento, 1998.
David, Charles Wendell, ed. *De Expugnatione Lyxbonensi*. New York: Columbia University Press, 1936.
Duby, Georges. *The Legend of Bouvines: War, Religion and Culture in the Middle Ages*. Berkeley, CA; and Los Angeles, CA: University of California Press, 1990.
Edgington, Susan B. 'The Capture of Lisbon: Premeditated or Opportunistic?'. In *The Second Crusade: Holy War on the Periphery of Latin Christendom*. Eds. Jason T. Roche and Janus Møller Jensen. Turnhout: Brepols, 2015, pp. 257–72.
Emery, Elizabeth and Laura Morowitz. *Consuming the Past: The Medieval Revival in fin-de-siècle France*. Aldershot: Ashgate, 2003.
Erdmann, Carl. *Die Entstehung des Kreuzzugsgedankens*. Stuttgart: W. Kohlhammer, 1935.
———. *O Papado e Portugal no primeiro século da história portuguesa*. Translated by João da Providência e Costa. Coimbra: Instituto Alemão da Universidade de Coimbra, 1935.
———. *A idea de cruzada em Portugal*. Translated by Arménio Ferreira Pinto Carvalho. Coimbra: Instituto Alemão da Universidade de Coimbra, 1940.
Hobsbawm, Eric. 'Mass-Producing Traditions: Europe, 1870–1914'. In *The Invention of Tradition*. Eds. Eric Hobsbawm and Terence Ranger. Cambridge: Cambridge University Press, 1983, pp. 263–307.
João, Maria Isabel. *Memória e Império. Comemorações em Portugal (1880–1960)*. Lisbon: FCG/FCT, 2002.
Leal, Ernesto Castro. 'Comemorações, poderes e espectáculo: o VIII Centenário da Tomada de Lisboa aos Mouros em 1947'. In *I Colóquio Temático O Município de Lisboa e a Dinâmica Urbana (sécs. XVI-XX)*. Lisbon: Câmara Municipal de Lisboa, 1998, pp. 473–96.
———. *Nação e Nacionalismos. A Cruzada Nacional D. Nuno Álvares Pereira e as origens do Estado Novo (1918–1938)*. Lisbon: Cosmos, 1999.
———. 'Poder, Memória e Glória: comemoração do 8° centenário da tomada de Lisboa aos mouros'. *Revista Portuguesa de História* 36 (2002–2003), pp. 313–34.
———. 'Poder e comemoração: Festa do Patriotismo, Festa da Pátria em Portugal (1920–1938)'. *Turres Veteras* 8 (2006), pp. 275–83.
Matos, Sérgio Campos. 'O V Centenário Henriquino (1960): Portugal entre a Europa e o Império'. In *O Fim da Segunda Guerra Mundial e os novos rumos da Europa*. Ed. António José Telo. Lisbon: Cosmos, 1996, pp. 153–69.
———. 'D. Afonso Henriques na cultura histórica oitocentista'. In *2° Congresso Histórico de Guimarães*. Vol. 3. Guimarães: Câmara Municipal de Guimarães/ Universidade do Minho, 1997, pp. 233–48.
Mattoso, José. 'Perspectivas actuais da investigação e da síntese na historiografia medieval portuguesa (1128–1383)'. *Revista de História Económica e Social* 9 (1982), pp. 145–62.
———. 'No 850° aniversário da conquista de Lisboa'. *Arqueologia Medieval* 7 (2001), pp. 11–13.

Neto, Maria João Baptista. *Memória, Propaganda e Poder: O Restauro dos Monumentos Nacionais (1929–1960)*. Porto: FAUL Publicações, 2001.

Phillips, Jonathan. 'St Bernard of Clairvaux, The Low Countries and the Lisbon Letter of the Second Crusade'. *The Journal of Ecclesiastical History* 48 (1997), pp. 485–97.

———. 'Ideas of Crusade and Holy War in *De Expugnatione Lyxbonensi* (The Conquest of Lisbon)'. *Studies in Church History* 36 (2000), pp. 123–41.

Roche, Jason T. 'The Second Crusade: Main Debates and New Horizons'. In. *The Second Crusade: Holy War on the Periphery of Latin Christendom*. Eds. Jason T. Roche and Janus Møller Jensen. Turnhout: Brepols, 2015, pp. 1–32.

Rosas, Fernando. *Portugal entre a Paz e a Guerra, 1939–1945. Estudo do impacte da II Guerra Mundial na economia e na sociedade portuguesas (1939–1945)*. Lisbon: Estampa, 1990.

———. 'O 14 de Agosto. As Aljubarrotas do Estado Novo'. *História* 3 (1998), pp. 46–53.

Schweizer. Stefan. *'Unserer Weltanschauung sichtbaren Ausdruck geben': nationsozialistische Geschichtsbilder in historischen Festzügen zum 'Tag der Deutschen Kunst'*. Göttingen: Wallstein, 2007.

Vakil, Abdoolkarim. 'From the *Reconquista* to *Portugal Islâmico*: Islamic Heritage in the Shifting Discourses of Portuguese Historiography and National Identity'. *Arqueologia Medieval* 8 (2003), pp. 5–17.

Ventura, António. 'A contestação ao Centenário Antoniano de 1895'. *Lusitania Sacra* 8–9 (1996–1997), pp. 361–83.

Wilson, Jonathan. 'Enigma of the *De Expugnatione Lyxbonensi*'. *Journal of Medieval Iberian Studies* 9 (2017), pp. 99–129.

2 The Tsar's Crusade
Invented Holy War Tradition in Russia (1780–1920)

Adam Knobler

Russian holy war is a thoroughly unexplored field; scholars cannot even decide if Orthodoxy has a notion of holy war at all. Some, such as Athēna Kolia-Dermitzakē and Tia Kolbaba, seem to have concluded that there was.[1] Others, such as John Haldon and Warren Treadgold, seem just as convinced there was no such notion in Byzantium, the latter stating that, '[a]mong the Byzantines no wars were holy'.[2] For Russia, which followed in the Byzantine Orthodox tradition, holy war is thus largely a phenomenon without genuine precedent, and Russian crusading is without any medieval basis. The argument of this chapter is based on the notion that the Russians invented holy war based on a Western model in the late eighteenth century. I contend that a certain strain of ultra-conservatism in Russian thought blended with Western crusading imagery and ideology which couched much of the Russian warfare against the Ottoman Empire and other enemies in the long nineteenth century in crusading terms.

I have detailed at some length elsewhere the circumstances which developed into the use of holy war and crusade rhetoric in the long nineteenth century.[3] Conservative semiotic alternatives to the symbolism of revolution, which would find easy translation into popular media, were of the utmost importance. Russia, which did not face a revolutionary or liberal surge in the nineteenth century, looked upon its self-appointed role as the last bulwark of Christendom, in opposition to Western Europe's failure to meet anti-Christian threats, as a pulpit from which to preach holy war.[4] Russia's foil was not, thus, liberals at home, but the West, broadly defined. In Russia, Slavophils, who had never been comfortable with the Western orientation of some members of court, could thus adopt a Western notion – crusading – while still rejecting Western attitudes and mores.

An eighteenth-century collection of Greek prophetic sources, *Agathangelos*, repeatedly cites prophecies which envision a specifically

DOI: 10.4324/9781003241935-3

Russian restoration of Byzantium.⁵ The collection was widely disseminated in Greece and especially among Greek communities abroad, and it went into a number of editions, through the 1910s.⁶ The sizeable Greek community in exile in Russia must have known of them, and it would then make sense to look at the rather prominent role Byzantium played in Russian thought at this time.

We can see hints of this type of Philhellenism in Catherine the Great's so-called Greek Project.⁷ First advanced in the late 1770s by Prince Alexander Bezborodko, the plan, arranged between Catherine and the Habsburg Emperor Joseph II, was to divide the Ottoman Empire between them, and to install Catherine's grandson (and Paul's son) the appropriately (and intentionally) named Konstantin, as a new Byzantine Emperor. In fact, a medal was struck in honour of his birth in 1779, which bore the inscription 'Back to Byzantium'.⁸ He was even given a Greek nursemaid, named Helen and taught the Greek language before he was taught Russian.⁹ This Philhellenism extended to other members of Catherine's inner circle. For example, royal favourite Prince Grigory Potemkin gave Greek names to a series of new towns in Ukraine, including Odessa (after Odessos), Kherson (after Chersonesus), and Sevastopol.¹⁰ The project was called off due to Joseph's death in 1790 and Russian economic inability to see the plan through.

Tsar Paul I, son and heir of Catherine the Great, assumed the Grand Mastership of the Knights Hospitaller following the fall of Malta to Napoleon in 1798.¹¹ Paul, who began to be interested in the knights at the age of ten, held a fascination for royal martyrs of the West, and, based on his reading of the Abbé de Vertot's *Histoire des chevaliers hospitaliers* of 1726, saw in the aristocratic chivalry of the knights an opportunity to introduce to Russia Western pomp, pride and ceremony which he thought distinctly lacking in the Russian nobility.¹² Constructing his Michael's Palace (*Mikhailovskii zamok*) in Saint Petersburg with a grand meeting hall for the Knights, Paul saw a direct connection between Western crusading and Russian noble revival.¹³ Paul's fascination with crusading was taken by his contemporaries to be a sign of his mental instability.¹⁴ The nobility, for whom he had such lavish headquarters constructed, were fundamentally opposed to being Westernised in such a fashion, and had him assassinated in 1801.

The notion of re-establishing the Byzantine Empire became central to the thought of many pan-Orthodox and pan-Slav advocates in eastern Europe and Russia throughout the nineteenth century and into the beginnings of the twentieth. Fervent in this regard, was the Slavophil historian Mikhail Pogodin (1800–75), who stated that 'As Orthodox Christians, we must [...] return to Saint Sophia its ecumenical cross.'¹⁵ The romantic poet,

Fyodor Tyutchev, in 1848 wrote a poem entitled 'Russian Geography' which spoke of 'Constantine's city', meaning Constantinople, as a holy capital of the Russian realm alongside Moscow and St. Petersburg; a realm which stretched from the 'Elbe to China' and from 'the Ganges to the Danube'.[16] In his poem 'Prophecy' (1850), he wrote of the Tsar constructing an altar in Byzantium.[17] This idea, of a Russian Byzantium, as we shall see, continued through the First World War.

Shortly after Tyutchev produced his piece, Russia went to war with the Ottoman Empire again. The Crimean War (1853–56) ostensibly began as a conflict concerning religion. Eastern Orthodox Christians dwelling in the Holy Land were supposed to be living under the protection of the Russian Empire. It was to be, for many, the opportunity for the enactment of Russia's world-historical mission. The Tsar, Nicholas I, eventually demanded that all Orthodox Christians in the Ottoman Empire were to be placed under Russian protection. In response, the British and French, not wanting the Tsar to expand his power at the expense of the Ottomans, supported Sultan Abdülmecid I (r. 1839–61) when he declared war against Russia in October 1853. In 1854, Britain and France entered the fray. Orthodoxy was posited as the source of Russian inspiration, and the modern British historian of Russia Orlando Figes subtitled his book on the Crimean War as 'The Last Crusade'.[18] Likewise, Russian thinkers, such as Ivan Kireevskii, the philosopher of Slavophilism, saw the war as a Catholic versus Orthodox holy struggle.[19] The metaphor of the last crusade was made manifest in the sermons of Archbishop Innokentii of Kherson and Tauride and Metropolitan Filaret of Moscow.[20] They characterised the Orthodox Christians of the Ottoman Empire as desirous of rescue, and the war was proclaimed a holy war against Islam.

Nineteenth-century Russian historians themselves were not above making the connection. The ultra-conservative historian Stepan Shevyrev (1806–64), stated in 1853 that 'From all of Russia there is sympathy for the war [...] It is a crusade.'[21] Russian Orthodoxy became synonymous with the Russian state and Russian patriotism. Tsar Nicholas I (r. 1825–55) wrote to King Friedrich Wilhelm IV of Prussia (r. 1840–61) on 29 June 1854: 'Waging war neither for worldly advantages nor for conquests, but for a solely Christian purpose, must I be left alone to fight under the banner of the Holy Cross and to see the others, who call themselves Christians, all unite around the Crescent to combat Christendom?'[22] Thus, rhetoric in Russia identifying the Crimean War as a holy religious war comparable to the crusades existed at many levels of the society.

The nineteenth-century war in which the theme of holiness appeared most vividly, however, was the Russo-Turkish War of 1877–78. Dmitrii

Miliutin, the Russian Minister of War, stated that the death of Balkan Christians, notably in Bulgaria, at the hands of Turkish barbarism should be a call to arms for all Christian nations, notably France, Italy, and England.[23] In this he was recognising the west's history of holy war, and making parallels to Russia's own ambitions. Fyodor Dostoyevski (1821–81) wrote extensively about the necessity of restoring the Byzantine Empire at this time, and of the superiority of Russian Orthodoxy over all other forms of Christianity: '[S]ooner or later, Constantinople must be ours [...] as a leader of Orthodoxy' he wrote.[24] Dostoyevski, in the same piece, inveighed against both Islam and Western Europe, stating in essence that Russia and Orthodoxy would follow a separate, third path. Even non-Russians embraced the crusading parallel for this fight. The American observer Francis Greene (1850–1921), who was a young War Department attaché to St. Petersburg and served in the Russian army during the war with the Ottomans, gave a Western notion of the Russian situation writing that 'No more generous or holy crusade was ever undertaken on the part of a strong race to befriend a weak one.'[25]

The First World War was also referred to as a holy war in Russian popular media, and as a crusade by some churchmen.[26] While not as replete as in earlier wars, religiously themed *lubki* ('popular prints') continued to couch Russia in the symbols of Orthodoxy.[27] See, for example, Fig. 2.1, entitled 'Holy War', from 1914. The caption calls on *moguchaia Rus'* ['mighty Rus'] to pray 'that the deeds of our highest God lead us to victory until the end.' The image in this particular *lubok* is Tsar Nicholas II (r. 1894–1917) in the guise of a *bogatyr*: a medieval knight-errant, taken from folk stories or *byliny*. The *bogatyr* plays a significant role in Russian tradition, symbolising the indomitable national spirit, and personified by individuals such as the semi-legendary Ilya Muromets, and those who served with the warrior saint, Alexander Nevsky in the thirteenth century against Teutonic and Swedish invaders.[28] *Bogatyrs* feature prominently in *lubki* throughout the nineteenth and into the twentieth century.[29] Here, we can see how the Russian *bogatyr* warrior, like the military saint, parallels the Western sainted crusader: Alexander Nevsky and Louis IX of France. A Russian image put to a Western purpose – holy war.

As stated earlier, imagery of the fall of Constantinople/Istanbul also continued to find appeal among the Russian public during the First World War. For example, the 1915 Russian propaganda film, *Enver Pasha, The Traitor of Turkey*, ended with a dreamt image of a golden cross appearing atop the Hagia Sophia.[30] The Turks were not, of course, the only Islamic enemies of the Orthodox Russians. One could also include Tatars, Kazakhs, Dagestanis, Azeris, Uzbeks, and

The Tsar's Crusade   49

Figure 2.1   Tsar Nicholas II in the guise of a *bogatyr*; 'Holy War', 1914.
Source: Poster Collection, RU/SU 133, Hoover Institution Archives.

Turkmens among others. And while the holy war imagery for the conquest of Central Asia and the Muslim Caucasus was rather muted, the missionary activity such conquests spawned was often couched in crusading terms. The 1842 reopening of the Kazan Theological Academy, which was designated to prepare Orthodox clergy for mission in the East, was proclaimed by its secretary, as marking 'the dawn of a crusade'.[31] The word used, *krestonosnoe* is very specific – this is Westernstyle crusading. *Krestonosets*, meaning 'crusader', does not appear in the Russian language earlier than 1792.[32]

Islam was not the only enemy of Russia against whom holy war was aimed: the juxtaposition of a civilised Christendom to that of the Satan-inspired barbarous Japanese and Chinese also lent itself to imagery that, while not obviously crusading in the strictest of terms, certainly posited a holy battle to protect the faith. The idea of a repeat of the Mongol invasion, this time led by the Japanese, was voiced by philosopher Vladimir Solovyov (1853–1900), speaking of the 'Yellow Peril'. He spoke at length about a concept of pan-Mongolism, where Chinese and Japanese forces would unite to seize power in Europe.[33] German Kaiser Wilhelm II wrote to his cousin, Tsar Nicholas II, on several occasions, about the need to defend the Cross against the inroads of Buddhism – the implication was that 'Willy' had specific ideas about 'Nicky's' holy war sympathies.[34] When war did come against the Japanese in 1904, it was presented both as a racial war and as a holy war. Tsar Nicholas II issued a manifesto and prayers calling on God's support in gaining victory. On 4 August 1904, the Holy Synod called for prayers asking victory for Russia's 'Christ-loving troops'.[35]

Finally, holy war could be waged internally as well as against external enemies of Mother Russia. Here, we have evidence from the Russian Civil War of the early 1920s, where members of the White Army in Siberia established Military Orders, dubbed by the Bolsheviks as 'Regiments of Jesus' along the lines of their Western medieval counterparts, with names such as the Order of the Holy Cross. Curiously enough, such religious military units of Christian *and* Muslim troops were referred to in general by the Whites as 'Crossbearers'.[36]

Conclusion

Several elements seem to have found their nexus in these events. The first is a variety of Pan-Slavism, indeed Pan-Orthodoxy, which placed Russia at the centre of world events, and wherein Russia posited itself as the bulwark of Christianity against the non-Christian world, whether they be Turk, Persian, Chinese, or Japanese. The threat was always couched in religious terms – an assault on Christianity. The Bolsheviks, too, were condemned for their anti-religious stance.

This particular variety of Slavophilism paralleled a certain strain in Philhellenism, which developed among Greeks and others at the same time. The Russians were certain of their destiny to restore the Byzantine Empire, because, in part at least, the Greeks themselves deemed it to be so. The failure of the Greek Project was just a mere glitch, to be continued by future generations of Orthodox Russians acting as the Third Rome, the successor to Byzantium, eventually restoring the Second Rome to its rightful place. It is interesting to note that copies of the *Agathangelos* were produced at the opening of both the Crimean War and the First World War.

The Tsar's Crusade 51

As opposed to Westernisation as the most radical of Slavophils were, there was also a sense that the Latins had established a legal framework within which the defence of coreligionists was seen as a suitable justification for the declaration of a war as holy, just and righteous. This was clearly picked up by the Russians who noted rather disappointingly that the other Christian nations of Europe were not carrying on the holy war traditions as they should be and were not opposing those who posed a threat to Christendom. This Western crusading, which found a place in the Russian language in the late eighteenth century, was given an Orthodox spin. While we can consider Paul I's rather quirky flirtation with the Hospitallers something of an anomaly (the Knights had, after all, not been an effective crusading fighting force for more than a century), its primary fault was that it was *too* Western for the Russian nobility.

This is not to say that the Russians wholly rejected an interest in Latin crusading. Western books on crusading, ranging from Auguste Gruson's history of the crusades for children (translated into Russian in 1844) to Michaud's grand *Histoire* (translated in 1884) were widely available in Russia.[37] What we thus begin to see is a curious mixture of Western holy war ideology and ultra conservative Slavophilism, what the Russians would call *pochvennichestvo* meaning 'return to the soil'. Holy war ideology in the nineteenth century, as I have argued elsewhere, was very much the province of ultra conservatives, so perhaps we should not be so surprised to see vehemently anti-European, anti-Western conservatives in Russia taking up holy war imagery as a natural course of Russian events, even if they might wish to deny a Western origin to the process.[38] As a final observation, the recent 2022 Russian invasion of Ukraine has been couched in holy war terms by both President Vladimir Putin and Russian Patriarch Kirill.[39] Whoever thought the long nineteenth century would last so long indeed?

Notes

1 Athēna Kolia-Dermitzakē, *Ho Vyzantinos 'hieros polemos': he ennoia kai e provole tou threskeutikou polemou sto Vyzantio* (Athens, 1991); Tia M. Kolbaba, 'Fighting for Christianity: Holy War in the Byzantine Empire', *Byzantion* 68 (1998), pp. 194–221.
2 John Haldon, *Warfare, State and Society in the Byzantine World, 565–1204* (London, 1999); Warren Treadgold, 'Byzantium, the Reluctant Warrior', in *Noble Ideals and Bloody Realities*, eds. Niall Christie and Maya Yazigi (Leiden, 2006), p. 212.
3 See Knobler, 'Holy Wars'.

4 See letter of Nicholas I to Friedrich Wilhelm below; also see Dmitrii Alekseevich Miliutin, *Vospominaniia* (Newtonville, MA, 1979).
5 *Ho Agathangelos, ētoi, Prophēteiai peri tou mellontos tōn ethnōn, kai idiōs peri tēs Hellados: hoptasia eranistheisa ek palaiōn cheirographōn met' akrivous hermēneias holōn tōn symvēsomenōn*, 8th edn. (Athens, n.d.).
6 See John Nicolopoulos, 'From Agathangelos to the Megale Idea: Russia and the Emergence of Modern Greek nationalism', *Balkan Studies* 26 (1985), pp. 41–56.
7 On the Greek Project, see Hugh Ragsdale, 'Evaluating the Traditions of Russian Aggression: Catherine II and the Greek Project', *Slavonic and East European Review* 66 (1988), pp. 91–117; David M. Griffiths, 'Greek Project', in *The Modern Encyclopedia of Russian and Soviet History*, vol. 13, ed. Joseph L. Wieczynski (Gulf Breeze, 1979), pp. 128–32. Maya Kucherskaya, 'Grand Duke Constantine Pavlovich Romanov in Russian Cultural Mythology' (PhD dissertation, UCLA, 1999), chap. 2.
8 On the coin / medal, Kucherskaya, 'Grand Duke Constantine', p. 54.
9 On Konstantin's youth and education, see Maiia Kuchersakaia, *Konstantin Pavlovich* (Moscow, 2005), chap. 1.
10 On Greek place names in Imperial Russia, see 'Rossiiskie goroda s grecheskimi imenami', *Sevatopolskaya Gazeta*, 20 July 2006, <http://sevastopol.press/2006/07/20/vopros-otvet>, [accessed 16 December 2016].
11 On Paul and the Hospitallers, see Vladimir Zakharov, *Imperator Pavel I i Orden sviatogo Ioanna Ierusalimskogo* (St. Petersburg, 2007); *Imperator Pavel Pervyi I Orden Sv. Ioanna Ierusalimskogo v Rossii: sbornik Statei*, ed. R. Krasiukov (St. Petersburg, 1995); Michel A. Taube, *L'empereur Paul Ier de Russie, Grand Maître de l'Ordre de Malte et son 'Grand Prieuré Russe' de l'Ordre de Saint-Jean-de-Jérusalem* (Geneva, 1982); Roderick E. McGrew, 'Paul I and the Knights of Malta', in *Paul I: A Reassessment of His Life and Reign*, ed. Hugh Ragsdale (Pittsburgh, PA, 1979), pp. 44–75.
12 On Paul's early reading, see Roderick E. McGrew, *Paul I of Russia, 1754–1801* (New York, NY, 1992), p. 259.
13 On the Michael Palace, see M.B. Asvarishch, *Mikhailovskii zamok* (St. Petersburg, 2004); Liudmila Veniaminovna, 'Mikhailovskii Zamok i Nektorye Aspekty Religiozno-Filofskikh Vozzrenii Pavla I', *Otechestvennaia Istoriia* 2 (2000), pp. 164–70.
14 Charles Whitworth, the British ambassador to St. Petersburg, thought Paul's fondness for pomp was a waste of time, and stated so in a letter to British Foreign Secretary Grenville. See FO/65/38 no. 64, 14 December 1797, St. Petersburg, TNA. On Paul's supposed mental instability, see Hugh Ragsdale, *Tsar Paul and the Question of Madness* (New York, NY, 1988).
15 M.P. Pogodin, *Sochineniia M P Pogodina, IV: Istoriko-politicheskiia pis'ma i zapiski v prodolzhenii k krymskoi voiny, 1853–1856*, ed. Nikolai Barsukov (Moscow, 1874). Nicholas V. Riasanovsky, 'Pogodin and Sevyrev in Russian Intellectual History', *Harvard Slavic Studies* 4 (1957), pp. 149–67.
16 F.I. Tyutchev, *Poems & Political Letters of F.I. Tyutchev*, trans. Jesse Zeldin (Knoxville, TN, 1973), p. 131.
17 See Frank L. Fadner, *Seventy Years of Pan-Slavism in Russia* (Washington, DC, 1962), p. 283.

18 Orlando Figes, *Crimea: The Last Crusade* (London, 2010).
19 Peter K. Christoff, *An Introduction to Nineteenth-Century Russian Slavophilism: Vol. 2: Kireevskij* ('s-Gravenhage, 1961–91), p. 257.
20 See sermons of both: Innokentii, 'Rech' po prochtenii vysochaishago manifesta o voine s turtsieiu', in his *Sochineniia* 8 (St. Petersburg, 1874), p. 9; idem., 'Slovo pri poseshchenii pastavy', in *Sochineniia* 2 (St. Petersburg, 1908), p. 239; Filaret in *Zhizn i Trudy M P Pogodina*, ed. Nikolai Barsukov (St. Petersburg, 1899), 3, p. 9. In general, see Mara Kozelsky, *Christianizing Crimea* (DeKalb, IL, 2010), chap. 5.
21 Letter from S.P. Shevyrev to M.P. Pogodin, 25 December 1853 in *Zhizn i Trudy MP Pogodina* (St. Petersburg, 1888–1910), 13, pp. 18–19; see, too, Olga Maiorova, *From the Shadow of Empire* (Madison, 2010), p. 30.
22 See letter of Nicholas I to Friedrich Wilhelm IV, Theodor Schiemann, *Geschichte Russlands unter Kaiser Nikolaus I*, 4 vols. (Berlin, 1904–19), 4, pp. 430.
23 Miliutin, *Vospominaniia*.
24 Fyodor Dostoyevski, *Dnevnik Pisatelia za 1877 god* (Paris, 1951), March 1877, p. 97. Idem., *The Diary of a Writer*, trans. Boris Brasol, 2 vols. (London, 1949), 1, p. 362; 2, p. 626.
25 Francis V. Greene, *Sketches of Army Life in Russia* (New York, NY: Scribner's, 1880), ch. 1, sect. 14.
26 'This war must be looked upon as a holy crusade', remarked Archbishop Arsenii of Khar'kov in July 1914. See Gosudarstvennyi Sovet, *Stenograficheskii Otchet*, ix Session 20 July 1914, cols. 5–6 cited by John Shelton Curtiss, *Church and State in Russia* (New York, NY, 1972), p. 381.
27 See Norris, *War of Images*, pp. 146–52.
28 James Bailey and Tatyana Ivanova, *An Anthology of Russian Folk Epics* (London, 1998), pp. 25–80; Mari Isoaho, *The Image of Aleksandr Nevskiy in Medieval Russia* (Leiden, 2006). See, too, the bogatyr paintings of Victor Vasnetsov (1848–1926).
29 See, for example, the *lubok* entitled 'The Russian Bogatyr' in the East' in Norris, *War of Images*, p. 122.
30 On Enver Pasha see Hubertus F. Jahn, *Patriotic Culture in Russia During World War I* (Ithaca, 1996), pp. 162–63.
31 Petr Vasil'evich Znamenskii, *Istoriia Kazanskoi dukhovnoi akademii za pervyi (doreformennoi) period eia sush, vaniia (1842–1870 gody)* (Kazan, 1891–92), p. 21.
32 On similar words, see *Slovar' russkogo iazyka 'XVIII' veka*, ed. I.U.S. Sorokin, vol. 11 (Leningrad, 1984).
33 See Susanna Soojung Lim, *China and Japan in the Russian Imagination 1685–1922* (London, 2015); Vladimir Solov'ev, 'Kitai i Evropa', *Sobranie sochinenii Vladimira Solov'eva*, eds. S.M. Solov'ev and E. Radlov, 12 vols. (Brussels, 1966–70), 6, pp. 84–137. Vladimir Solov'ev, 'Panmongolizm', at <http://max.mmlc.northwestern.edu/mdenner/Demo/texts/panmongolism.html>, [accessed 4 June 2017]. On Solov'ev and the Far East, see Susanna Soojung Lim, 'Between Spiritual Self and Other: Vladimir Solov'ev and the Question of East Asia', *Slavic Review* 67 (2008), pp. 321–41; David Schimmelpenninck van der Oye, *Toward the Rising Sun* (DeKalb, IL, 2001), pp. 82–86.

34 Wilhelm II to Nicholas, letters, 10 June 1895 and 26 September 1895, in Isaac Don Levine, ed., *Letters from the Kaiser to the Czar* (New York, NY, 1920), pp. 12–15, 17.
35 John Shelton Curtiss, *Church and State in Russia, 1900–1917* (New York, NY, 1965), p. 78; *Tserkovnyia Vedomosti*, 28 August 1904, official part, p. 386; Rosamund Bartlett, 'Japonisme and Japanophobia: The Russo-Japanese War in Russian Cultural Consciousness', *The Russian Review* 67 (2008), pp. 8–33.
36 Noted in John Shelton Curtiss, *The Russian Church and the Soviet State, 1917–1950* (Gloucester, 1965), p. 99; see also Anton Ivanovich Denikin, *Ocherki Russkoi Smuty*, 5 vols. (Paris, 1921–26), 5, pp. 157–58.
37 Russian translations of crusade histories: Auguste Gruson, *Istorīia krestovykh pokhodov v razskazakh dlia dietei s kartinami* (St. Petersburg, V tip. Shtaba otd. korp. vnutrenneii strazhi, 1849) and Joseph François Michaud, *Istoriia krestovykh pokhodov* (St. Petersburg: Izd. t-va M.O. Volf, 1884). The Western and eastern are discussed in G. Titov's 1854 anti-Western pamphlet *Krestovye pokhody i Vostochnyi vopros* (St. Petersburg: Voennaia tip., 1854). Thanks to Ol'ga Saposnikova for finding this pamphlet for me in St. Petersburg and to Zara Pogossian for providing me with a summary translation.
38 Knobler, 'Holy Wars'.
39 Paul Elie, 'The Long Holy War behind Putin's political war in Ukraine', *New Yorker*, 21 April 2022, <https://www.newyorker.com/news/daily-comment/the-long-holy-war-behind-putins-political-war-in-ukraine>, [accessed 26 April 2022]; Jack Jenkins, 'How One Priest turned Putin's invasion into a Holy War', *Rolling Stone*, 19 March 2022, <https://www.rollingstone.com/politics/politics-features/holy-war-priest-putin-war-ukraine-1323914/>, [accessed 26 April 2022]. Charles P. Pierce, 'Russia's Assault on Ukraine has a Crusader element', *Esquire*, 24 February 2022, <https://www.esquire.com/news-politics/politics/a39212527/russia-ukraine-orthodox-christianity-crusade/> [accessed 26 April 2022].

Bibliography

Archival

FO/65/38 no. 64, 14 December 1797, St. Petersburg, TNA.

Primary

Bailey, James, and Tatyana Ivanova. *An Anthology of Russian Folk Epics*. London: M.E. Sharpe, 1998.
Denikin, Anton Ivanovich. *Ocherki Russkoi Smuty*. 5 Vols. Paris: Rodnik, 1921–26.
Dostoyevski, Fyodor. *The Diary of a Writer*. trans. Boris Brasol. 2 Vols. London: Cassell, 1949.
———. *Dnevnik Pisatelia za 1877 god*. Paris: YMCA Press, 1951.
Filaret, *Zhizn i Trudy M P Pogodina, ed. Nikolai Barsukov*. Vol. 3. St. Petersburg: Stasliulevicha, 1899.

Greene, Francis V. *Sketches of Army Life in Russia*. New York: Scribner's, 1880.

Ho Agathangelos, *ētoi, Prophēteiai peri tou mellontos tōn ethnōn, kai idiōs peri tēs Hellados: hoptasia eranistheisa ek palaiōn cheirographōn met' akrivous hermēneias holōn tōn symvēsomenōn*. 8th edn. Athens: Saliberou, n.d.

Innokentii. 'Rech' po prochtenii vysochaishago manifesta o voine s turtsieiu', in *Sochineniia* 8. St. Petersburg: Tuzov, 1874, p. 9.

———. 'Slovo pri poseshchenii pastavy'. In *Sochineniia* 2. St. Petersburg: Tuzov, 1908, p. 239.

Levine, Isaac Don ed. *Letters from the Kaiser to the Czar*. New York: Frederick A. Stokes, 1920.

Pogodin, M.P. *Sochineniia M P Pogodina, IV: Istoriko-politicheskiia pis'ma i zapiski v prodolzhenii k krymskoi voiny, 1853–1856*. ed. Nikolai Barsukov. Moscow: VM Frish, 1874.

———. *Zhizn i Trudy MP Pogodina*. St. Petersburg: Tip. MM Stasiulevicha, 1888–1910.

Schiemann, Theodor. *Geschichte Russlands unter Kaiser Nikolaus I*. 4 Vols. Berlin: Reimer, 1904–19.

Solov'ev, Vladimir. 'Kitai i Evropa'. In *Sobranie sochinenii Vladimira Solov'eva*. eds. S.M. Solov'ev and E. Radlov. 12 Vols. Brussels: Foyer Oriental Chrétien, 1966–70.

Titov, G. *Krestovye pokhody i Vostochnyi vopros*. St. Petersburg: Voennaia tip., 1854.

Tyutchev, F.I. *Poems & Political Letters of F.I. Tyutchev*. trans. Jesse Zeldin. Knoxville, TN: University of Tennessee Press, 1973.

Znamenskii, Petr Vasil'evich. *Istoriia Kazanskoi dukhovnoi akademii za pervyi (doreformennoi) period eia sush, vaniia (1842–1870 gody)*. Kazan: Tip. Imp. Universiteta, 1891–92.

Secondary

Asvarishch, M.B. *Mikhailovskii zamok*. St. Petersburg: Beloe i Chernoe, 2004.

Christoff, Peter K. *An Introduction to Nineteenth-Century Russian Slavophilism: Vol. 2: Kireevskij*. 's-Gravenhage: Mouton, 1961–91.

Curtiss, John Shelton. *The Russian Church and the Soviet State, 1917–1950*. Gloucester: Peter Smith, 1965.

———. *Church and State in Russia: The Last Years of the Empire, 1900–1917*. New York: Octagon, 1972.

Fadner, Frank L. *Seventy Years of Pan-Slavism in Russia: Karazin to Danilevskii, 1800–1870*. Washington, DC: Georgetown University Press, 1962.

Figes, Orlando. *Crimea: The Last Crusade*. London: Allen Lane, 2010.

Griffiths, David M. 'Greek Project', in *The Modern Encyclopedia of Russian and Soviet History*. Vol. 13. Ed. Joseph L. Wieczynski. Gulf Breeze: Academic International Press, 1979, pp. 128–32.

Haldon, John. *Warfare, State and Society in the Byzantine World, 565–1204*. London: UCL Press, 1999.

Isoaho, Mari. *The Image of Aleksandr Nevskiy in Medieval Russia: Warrior and Saint*. Leiden: Brill, 2006.
Jahn, Hubertus F. *Patriotic Culture in Russia During World War I*. Ithaca, NY: Cornell University Press, 1996.
Knobler, Adam. 'Holy Wars, Empires, and the Portability of the Past: The Modern Uses of Medieval Crusades'. *Comparative Studies in Society & History* 48 (2006), pp. 293–325.
Kolbaba, Tia M. 'Fighting for Christianity: Holy War in the Byzantine Empire'. *Byzantion* 68 (1998), pp. 194–221.
Kolia-Dermitzakē, Athēna. *Ho Vyzantinos 'hieros polemos': he ennoia kai e provole tou threskeutikou polemou sto Vyzantio*. Athens: Basilopulos, 1991.
Kozelsky, Mara. *Christianizing Crimea: Shaping Sacred Space in the Russian Empire and Beyond*. DeKalb, IL: Northern Illinois University Press, 2010.
Krasiukov, R. ed. *Imperator Pavel Pervyi I Orden Sv. Ioanna Ierusalimskogo v Rossii: sbornik Statei*. St. Petersburg: Kul'tInform Press, 1995.
Kucherskaia, Maiia [Kucherskaya, Maya]. 'Grand Duke Constantine Pavlovich Romanov in Russian Cultural Mythology'. PhD dissertation, UCLA, 1999.
———. *Konstantin Pavlovich*. Moscow: Molodaiia gvardiia, 2005.
Lim, Susanna Soojung. 'Between Spiritual Self and Other: Vladimir Solov'ev and the Question of East Asia', *Slavic Review* 67 (2008), pp. 321–41.
———. *China and Japan in the Russian Imagination 1685–1922*. London: Routledge, 2015.
Maiorova, Olga. *From the Shadow of Empire*. Madison, WI: University of Wisconsin Press, 2010.
McGrew, Roderick E. 'Paul I and the Knights of Malta'. In *Paul I: A Reassessment of His Life and Reign*. ed. Hugh Ragsdale. Pittsburgh, PA: University of Pittsburgh, 1979, pp. 44–75.
———. *Paul I of Russia, 1754–1801*. New York: OUP, 1992.
Miliutin, Dmitrii Alekseevich. *Vospominaniia*. Newtonville, MA: Oriental Research Partners, 1979.
Nicolopoulos, John. 'From Agathangelos to the Megale Idea: Russia and the Emergence of Modern Greek Nationalism., *Balkan Studies* 26 (1985), pp. 41–56.
Norris, Stephen M. *A War of Images: Russian Popular Prints, Wartime Culture, and National Identity, 1812–1945*. DeKalb, IL: Northern Illinois University Press, 2006.
Ragsdale, Hugh. 'Evaluating the Traditions of Russian Aggression: Catherine II and the Greek Project'. *Slavonic and East European Review* 66 (1988), pp. 91–117.
———. *Tsar Paul and the Question of Madness: An Essay in History and Psychology*. New York: Greenwood Press, 1988.
Riasanovsky, Nicholas V. 'Pogodin and Sevyrev in Russian Intellectual History'. *Harvard Slavic Studies* 4 (1957), pp. 149–67.
Schimmelpenninck van der Oye, David. *Toward the Rising Sun*. DeKalb, IL: Northern Illinois University Press, 2001.

Sorokin, I.U.S. ed. *Slovar' russkogo iazyka 'XVIII' veka*. Vol. 11. Leningrad: Nauka, 1984.
Taube, Michel A. *L'empereur Paul Ier de Russie, Grand Maître de l'Ordre de Malte et son 'Grand Prieuré Russe' de l'Ordre de Saint-Jean-de-Jérusalem*. Geneva: Slatkine, 1982.
Treadgold, Warren. 'Byzantium, the Reluctant Warrior'. In *Noble Ideals and Bloody Realities: Warfare in the Middle Ages*. eds. Niall Christie and Maya Yazigi. Leiden: Brill, 2006, pp. 209–33.
Veniaminovna, Liudmila. 'Mikhailovskii Zamok i Nektorye Aspekty Religiozno-Filofskikh Vozzrenii Pavla I'. *Otechestvennaia Istoriia* 2 (2000), pp. 164–70.
Zakharov, Vladimir. *Imperator Pavel I i Orden sviatogo Ioanna Ierusalimskogo*. St. Petersburg: Aleteiia, 2007.

Online Articles

Elie, Paul. 'The Long Holy War behind Putin's political war in Ukraine'. *New Yorker*. 21 April 2022. https://www.newyorker.com/news/daily-comment/the-long-holy-war-behind-putins-political-war-in-ukraine. Accessed 26 April 2022.
Jenkins, Jack. 'How One Priest turned Putin's invasion into a Holy War'. *Rolling Stone*. 19 March 2022. https://www.rollingstone.com/politics/politics-features/holy-war-priest-putin-war-ukraine-1323914/. Accessed 26 April 2022.
Pierce, Charles P. 'Russia's Assault on Ukraine has a Crusader element'. *Esquire*. 24 February 2022. https://www.esquire.com/news-politics/politics/a39212527/russia-ukraine-orthodox-christianity-crusade/. Accessed 26 April 2022.
'Rossiiskie goroda s grecheskimi imenami'. *Sevatopolskaya Gazeta*. 20 July 2006. http://sevastopol.press/2006/07/20/vopros-otvet. Accessed 16 December 2016.
Solov'ev, Vladimir. 'Panmongolizm'. 1894. http://max.mmlc.northwestern.edu/mdenner/Demo/texts/panmongolism.html. Accessed 4 June 2017.

3 Perceptions of Crusader 'Athlit in Zionist Writing (1887–1941)

Judith Bronstein

Introduction

The 'tourist traffic' of the Frankish Kingdom was not confined to the legitimate participants of the large-scale and 'official' Crusades. Apart from these 'certificate holders', many thousands entered' the country annually [...] The Order of the Templars regarded the control of this immigration movement as one of its principal functions. It acted as a kind of Immigration Department for Crusaders [...] Pilgrims' Castle was not merely meant to denote that it was built by pilgrims. In point of fact, the Templars attached no particular value to the perpetuation of its origin. The name was meant to denote that it served as a quarantine station, a clearance camp for pilgrims. There is nothing new under the sun, even at 'Athlit.[1]

(Theodor F. Meysels, 1941)

This quotation is taken from a newspaper report written by the Jewish journalist and author Theodor F. Meysels, in 1941, for the *Palestine Post* (which in the 1950s became the *Jerusalem Post*). The *Post* was an English-language daily newspaper published in Jerusalem, which identified with the values and aims of the Zionist movement and its struggle for a Jewish homeland in Palestine.[2] This quotation regarding the purposes of the castle of 'Athlit and the tasks of the Knight Templars, exemplifies attitudes to the crusades and the crusaders in Zionist writing.

Much has been written on the utilisation of archaeological sites to bestow authenticity to religious and national claims.[3] Considering the Jewish and Zionist ideological attachment to the land, the question arises as to how historical sites which were culturally and religiously foreign to this discourse were perceived and interpreted. The present

DOI: 10.4324/9781003241935-4

Perceptions of Crusader 'Athlit in Zionist Writing (1887–1941) 59

study is part of ongoing research which examines the way in which crusade history and its material culture, which have no clear Jewish identification, were perceived, understood, interpreted and used in Zionist popular and scholarly writing in the early years of the Zionist movement. This new approach to the Zionist perception of crusader remains aims to shed light on the ways in which ideological and religious motivations affect how immigrant societies perceive and interpret their new environment. In this study I will demonstrate this by showing the changing perception of Zionist writers to the crusader castle of 'Athlit, from the late nineteenth century to the 1940s; that is, the period starting with the first Zionist settlement in Palestine to the end of the British mandate and the eve of the creation of the state of Israel. This was one of the most magnificent castles built in the Latin East in the thirteenth century, and is today an impressive remnant of the crusader period (Fig. 3.1).[4] Not only was this Templar castle prominent in the landscape, it was also located in close proximity to Zionist colonies established at the end of the nineteenth and the beginning

Figure 3.1 'Ruins of a Castle at Atlit', Z. Kluger, 1937/38.
Source: *Wikimedia Commons*.

of the twentieth century; it is visible from Zichron Ya'akov, located about twenty kilometres away from the castle, and the colony and later agricultural research station of 'Athlit is just a few kilometres away.[5] Due to its proximity and prominence the castle was often referred to in early Zionist popular and scholarly writing. This chapter aims to study changing patterns of perception and interpretation of the castle and its material remains.

Studies on the attitudes of Zionist writers to the crusader movement and the Latin East, from the end of the nineteenth to beginning of the twentieth century, tend to focus on three main topics: the fate of the Jewish communities; the Zionism-crusade analogy (especially between Israel and the crusader states); and related to this, the work of Joshua Prawer. Early Zionist literature suggests a negative perception of the crusades and the crusaders. The persecution of Jewish communities during the First Crusade, both in Europe and the Holy Land, affected the way in which the crusader period was perceived in Jewish historiography. Scholars tended to focus on the massacres of 1096 or on the fate of Jewish communities in Palestine during the crusader conquest.[6] Another focus of attention in popular and political as well as academic writing is that of the link between Zionism and the crusades. A parallel was drawn between the crusader movement and the Frankish kingdoms on the one hand and Zionism and the State of Israel on the other, considering both as Western colonial enterprises alien to the region with its religions, cultures, and customs. The implication was that as the first failed, so again would the second. Research conducted mainly by Israeli scholars in recent years has shown the ways this analogy was interpreted by Zionist writers, mainly used as a warning of past mistakes in order to guarantee the success of the Zionist enterprise. Related to this Zionism-crusade analogy is the work of Joshua Prawer, considered the founding father of crusader history in Mandatory Palestine, and later in the State of Israel. In a comprehensive study of the crusade motif in Israeli political discourse, Benjamin Z. Kedar has shown how Prawer aimed to differentiate the crusade movement and the crusader states from the Zionist project. Ronnie Ellenblum described the ways in which Prawer, in his prolific work extending from the late 1940s to the 1980s, considered the crusader period as a reverse prefiguration of the future Zionist movement; an anti-thesis to the Zionists' aims and achievements.[7]

The Zionism-crusade analogy and Prawer's work are the main approaches from which scholars have studied the topic of historical parallelism between the crusades and Zionism in recent decades. The starting point of most of these works is the late 1930s and 1940s,

Perceptions of Crusader 'Athlit in Zionist Writing (1887–1941)

almost fifty years after the beginning of the First Aliyah, the first Zionist immigration to Palestine. The rationale behind this starting point is that crusader studies conducted by Jewish scholars did not start before that. The crusader period had been considered peripheral to other historical periods and sites, which had a clear Jewish identification and would help to shape a national narrative and identity.[8] Although the focus of Zionist writers and scholars from the late nineteenth and most of the first half of the twentieth century was on Jewish material culture – on artefacts which strengthened the link between the Jewish past and the Jewish present in the Land of Israel – they also encountered remains from other cultures and periods, such as crusader castles and sites.

Early Zionist writers and 'Athlit

In a previous study I focused on the popular perception and interpretations of crusader material remains found in diaries and travel accounts of Zionist settlers and travellers in the first waves of Zionist immigration to Palestine in the late nineteenth and the early twentieth centuries. The analysis of these perceptions is significant because they represent the first encounter of this ideologically motivated nationalist immigration with the land and its physical remains. This analysis shows a diversity of emerging themes in the perception, interpretation and utilisation of crusader remains. Some settlers ignored them and referred in their writings only to Jewish sites. Others reflected on shattered remains of monasteries, towns and castles from the crusader period as symbolic evidence of the destruction of this culture; as evidence of the downfall of the Jew's past persecutors, in contrast to the endurance and revival of Jewish life. Some writers recontextualised crusader sites, whether consciously or unconsciously, into a Jewish narrative reflecting their search for roots and their attempt to connect to their new (but also ancient) home.[9]

Kalman Shlomo Kantor, for example, who moved to Palestine in 1887 and settled in the colony of Zichron Ya'akov, identified the Templar castle of 'Athlit, as Betar, the last stronghold of the Jewish final revolt against the Romans, a symbol of the Jewish glorified past, of the struggle for freedom and national independence. Although 'Athlit and Betar are two different sites, and Betar's location was not on the coast but a few kilometres south-west of Jerusalem, Kantor interpreted this monumental crusader castle as belonging to his own cultural and religious heritage. This perception of the crusader castle could have provided a tangible and visual representation of the Jewish heroic past, and enhanced the affinity with the land and its ancient heroes. Attitudes to the castle were, however, not uniform.

While Kantor interpreted the castle's remains as being part of a Jewish material heritage, other writers ignored the remains or dismissed them. Haim Hissin, who first immigrated to Palestine in 1882, toured the country with the aim of visiting newly founded Jewish colonies. But being an educated man with, so it seems from his writing, an interest in Jewish history, he also visited archaeological sites. He described his experience in his memoirs *Journey in the Promised Land* (*Masa' ba-Erets ha-mubtahat*), published as a series of articles in the 1890s in the Russian newspaper *Voshkod*.[10] Crusader material culture he encountered in Dor (the crusader castle of Merle) and Caesarea, were used by Hissin to reflect upon the endurance and resilience of the Jewish people and also his hopes for the success of the colonising enterprise.[11] Hissin seems to have been impressed with the remains of 'Athlit's castle, and he gave a detailed description of its walls, towers, and halls which, he wrote, were neglected and inhabited by peasants. And yet, probably because the site had no Jewish history known to him, Hissin attributed no importance to the castle's history: 'it is not known whether there was a town here in ancient times. All the ruins of 'Athlit belong to a newer period – the remains of the crusader castle, in spite of the little importance of the site, [...] are multiple and larger than those of Caesarea.'[12] While he was highly impressed with the remains of the latter city, he employed a critical tone in his description of 'Athlit: 'there is no need to describe these ruins – there is evidence in everything of a tendency for greatness that knows no bounds.'[13] Hissin commented that everything he saw demonstrated the crusaders' ambition 'for massiveness and grandeur.'[14] He made no attempt to understand the circumstances which led to these huge buildings, nor did he place the castle in its historical context. His emphasis was in the lands around the castle, not the castle itself; lands that were recently bought for Jewish colonisation. This is what, in his opinion, gave the site a history, and brought it to life.

The proximity of the castle to the Zionist colonies of Zichron Ya'akov and 'Athlit, and its prominence in the landscape, meant that it caught the attention of Zionist settlers and visitors more than any other crusader site in Palestine. As we have seen with Kantor, the ruins of the castle were visited. Short reports in Jewish newspapers refer to visits made to the site, unfortunately without giving more specific information about the purposes of the visit nor what kind of historical explanations were given at the site, if any. Thus, for example, in April 1921 Baron James Rothschild visited the Zionist settlement of Zichron

Perceptions of Crusader 'Athlit in Zionist Writing (1887–1941) 63

Ya'akov. Details of this visit was reported in the Jerusalem's Hebrew newspaper *Doar Hayom*, where it is also mentioned that the Baron, his entourage, and all the settlers 'young and old', went to visit 'old 'Athlit' without, however, giving any details regarding the site itself or its history.[15] The castle was mentioned in diaries and personal accounts of pioneers. In a letter of 1904, Judith Eisenberg (later Harari), a teacher who immigrated to Palestine with her family in 1886, wrote to her husband-to-be that on her way from Zichron Ya'akov to Haifa she visited the castle of 'Athlit. She gave a detailed description of the Jewish settlement of Zichron, and wrote that the castle was, 'an old castle from the time of the crusades. Inside the castle, deep in the ground are tunnels, stables for horses, and a cistern of running water.'[16] A pioneer working in the settlement of 'Athlit in 1921, known only by their initials Y.B., described the beauty of the place: 'The settlement is on a plain, the plain of 'Athlit which is only fifteen minutes' walk from the sea. Next to it stood the castle of 'Athlit, which was built by the crusaders.'[17]

The castle of 'Athlit, as explained above, was the crusader site most frequently referred to in the writings of the Zionist immigrants of the late nineteenth and early twentieth centuries. From these descriptions we can see that this crusader castle was an integral part of the settlers' landscape, but as was the case with Hissin, most accounts gave a separate description of the Jewish agricultural colonies of Zichron Ya'akov and 'Athlit and of the crusader castle, which they described briefly. They described two separate sites with no shared history.

'Athlit in the 1920s

An examination of some of the Zionist writing from the second decade of the twentieth century, however, shows an attempt to change this perception, to merge the site of the crusader castle with that of Jewish ancient and present history. This change was prompted mainly by the endeavour of immigrants of the second and third waves of immigration (known as the Second and Third Aliyah, 1904–23), Socialist-Zionists who saw in the creation of a national Hebrew culture an integral and essential component in the establishment of a Jewish homeland in Palestine. This received a great boost with the institution of British rule over Palestine through the League of Nations Mandate, which brought with it economic stability and, more relevant to our topic, a blossoming of scientific research in and on Palestine.[18]

From the 1920s a more proactive approach towards research, exploration and education was adopted by Zionist institutions, such as the 'Committee for Culture' of the General Federation of Labour (*Va'dat ha-tarbut' shel Histadrut ha-'ovdim*) and the Hebrew/Jewish Palestinian Exploration Society (*Hevrah ha-'Ivrit le-hakirat Erets Yisra'el ve-'atikoteah*). These institutions stressed the importance of education and culture, especially the field of *Yed'iat ha'arets* ('knowing/Learning the Land'). By studying and teaching all fields connected to the Land of Israel, such as history, geography, geology, botany, biology, and by promoting the Hebrew language, they aimed to support the Jewish material claim to the Land and to lend historical authenticity to the Zionist effort. Their works were also important in shaping a common identity that could be shared by Jews coming from very different countries and backgrounds. The collective past was used to bind these new migrants to each other and to their historical, and now actual, homeland.[19]

The castle of 'Athlit became a topic of study and interpretation by Zionist scholars and writers who used the site for their nationalist aims: to create an historical awareness attuned with the Zionist ideology. In 'The Land of Israel and Syria, a travel book' (*Erets Yisra'el ve-Suria ha-dromit, sefer masaot*) by Yeshayahu Press, the crusader site and the Jewish settlement became one. Press, who was the secretary of the newly founded Jewish Palestine Exploration Society, described in detail the crusader castle:

> 'Athlit was famous during the Crusades as the fortress of the immigrants (Château des Pélerins or Castelum Peregrinorum) [...] The Knights of the Temple fortified it well in 1218 and made it the centre of their order, which remained in their hands until it was destroyed in 1291 by the Sultan King Al-Ashraf [...] 'Athlit's position on a bedrock between two bays was well established. The outer wall had two towers and three gates from the east and one gate from the south. The channel that surrounded the wall on the land side was filled with seawater, and in the northeast were the remains of tower [...].

"Athlit', he added, 'is now a Hebrew colony founded in 1907 by the J.C.A. (Jewish Colonization association). It has 7,200 dunams of extensive pulse husbandry, and 108 residents.'[20]

Zionist scholars studied the crusader period and its archaeological remains to understand the country's physical and economic characteristics and to establish its geopolitical centrality. In his book *Haaretz* (*The Land of Israel*) of 1928, Abraham J. Brawer, a highly influential geographer, educator and one of the founding fathers of the Jewish

Palestine Exploration Society, examined several features which characterised the crusader kingdom. He placed a great emphasis on the role of the Land as a hub for international trade, and on the fact that the crusader kingdom enjoyed an economic boom, which expressed itself in intense building activity of castles, fortresses, churches, and monasteries 'wonderful buildings which can be seen until today.'[21] Brawer was concerned with the physical characteristics of the sites, for example he described 'Athlit as a place which, 'in the crusader period had a port and a castle by the name *castellum peregrinorum*. A small bay and a small extension of beach, a kind of peninsula which made this place a harbour for small boats for the crusaders.' He was also very impressed by the castle's ruins, which can still be seen from afar, up to the top of Mount Carmel. Like Press, Brawer continued his short description of the ruins with the area's modern history, stressing the establishment of the Jewish colony, the agricultural station and, after the Great War, the establishment of a salt industry at 'Athlit by the Palestine Jewish Colonization Association.[22]

'Athlit, as Ellenblum has shown in his analysis of T.E. Lawrence's book *Crusader Castles*, is an example of an ideological interpretation of a crusader castle which corresponded with British nationalist and colonialist discourses.[23] In this discourse, as demonstrated in Elizabeth Siberry's pioneering work, crusader imagery, perceptions and rhetoric had a central role.[24] This use of crusader medievalism for nationalistic purposes lead also, as shown by Mike Horswell in his recent study *The Rise and Fall of British Crusader Medievalism, c.1825–1945,* to an increased interest in crusader history and material remains. This was also reflected in initiatives calling for the preservation of crusader sites, including 'Athlit castle, which appeared in daily newspapers in Britain, in the 1920s. This increasing British interest mainly followed the establishment of the British Mandate over Palestine and coincides with the beginning of Zionist scholarly interest in the castle.[25]

'Athlit is therefore a fascinating case study also for the attitude of Zionist writers to crusader remains. Its prominence in the landscape, as stressed by Brawer, and its close proximity to Zionist settlements established at the end of the nineteenth century and at the beginning of the twentieth, such as Zichron Ya'akov and 'Athlit itself, meant that the castle of 'Athlit was an important topic of study and interpretation for Zionist writers who emphasised the Jewish roots of this impressive crusader castle, and determined its ancient Hebrew name. This was an important activity in which the Jewish Palestine Exploration Society, and many of its prominent members, including Brawer, were involved.[26]

An examination of the first proceedings of the Jewish Palestine Exploration Society of 1921 (in Hebrew) and 1925 (in English) reveals articles focusing almost exclusively on Jewish subjects.[27] These included reports of excavations conducted by members of the Society in Jerusalem, which studied Jewish burial sites (for example the Absalom Tomb), Hebrew inscriptions, and other Jewish remains dating mainly from the late Roman, Byzantine, and Arab periods. Outside Jerusalem they focused on material traces which could establish an uninterrupted Jewish presence upon the Land from the time of the destruction of the Second Temple to their present.[28] Although most of the scholarly writing on historical and archaeological sites from the beginning of the twentieth century dealt with Jewish sites, in the second issue of the Hebrew–language bulletin of the Jewish Palestine Exploration Society in 1921, Yitzhak Ben Zvi, one of the Society's founding fathers, an historian, Zionist leader, and Israel's second president, published an article entitled "Athlit, its name and Ancient Remains'. The article started with a short description of the ruins at 'Athlit and the history of the crusader castle: 'Perched on the Mediterranean coast and dominating the entire area to this day, this is where the glorious fortress of the "Pilgrims" was built by the Knights of the Templars.'[29] He mentioned the fact that the castle – of which a few buildings, towers, and walls were still standing – was only a mute testimony to its past, after being dismantled throughout the centuries and hit by an earthquake in 1837. But what interested Ben Zvi and provided the main focus of his article, were not the monumental crusader ruins, but smaller material remains which attested to the site's more ancient history. He identified the traces of salt mining as Khirbet Malha ('the ruins of the salt'), and a fragmentary rock inscription of large ancient characters found next to the castle as being possibly Semitic, and probably the first two or three letters of the name 'Athlit. Ben Zvi considered that these characters attested to the occupation of the site long before the arrival of the crusades and that 'Athlit was an ancient Hebrew name, deriving from the biblical 'Atali' or 'Athalia'. He considered that at least a thousand years before the crusaders built the castle a Jewish settlement existed by that name, dating from the time of the Second Temple or even from the time of Alexander the Great, a settlement which dwindled with the expansion of Christianity. The main occupation of the settlement was the salt industry he argued, as attested to by the archaeological and historical evidence.[30]

The fact that Ben Zvi's was one of the few articles in the first volume of the bulletin of the Jewish Palestine Exploration Society dealing with a seemingly non-Jewish site, is I believe, significant. While more popular writing and the personal accounts of pioneers referred to the archaeological site of 'Athlit and the new Jewish agricultural settlement as two separate entities with no shared history, Ben Zvi combined the two. He looked among the remnants of the crusader castle for material evidence which would link the pioneers with their old historical and, now, new land. These physical remains helped him to give the site, located in the midst of Zionist colonies, a concrete and tangible Jewish past. This historical explanation seems to have achieved its goal. A newspaper article on 'Athlit's quarries published in the Hebrew Palestinian newspaper *Davar* in 1931 explained about the precedence of the name 'Athlit: 'the scholars believe that in this place there was an ancient Hebrew settlement and the name 'Athlit was preserved from ancient times, from the name Athaliah bat 'Omri, the famous queen.'[31] Pertinent to this argument, is the fact that Ben Zvi's article on 'Athlit was included in his book *Sha'ar Yeshuv* (*Remnants of Ancient Hebrew Communities in the Land of Israel*) of 1927. In this book Ben Zvi painstakingly studied historical as well as material evidence to show an uninterrupted Jewish presence in the land throughout the centuries. The purpose was to establish an unbroken and unique Jewish historical connection with the land, a fundamental concept in Zionist ideology.[32]

The fact that Ben Zvi's article on the castle of 'Athlit was published in 1921 was unlikely to have been coincidental. That year the British government gave the Jewish Colonization Association a concession to mine salt in 'Athlit; this led to the creation of the Palestine Salt Company a year later. 'Another interesting point', wrote Ben Zvi, 'is the ruin of Malha (the ruins of salt), to the south of 'Athlit. Here, in ancient times, the salt was obtained, and like father like son; last year the Hebrew "Salt Company" started her activity in this salt flat area [...] here worked during the summer about twenty-five Hebrew workers.'[33] For Ben Zvi, the pioneers of the present continued the Jewish creativity of the past, realising the Zionist secular concept of 'redeeming' the land by physical presence and physical labour.[34]

Ben Zvi's article is highly significant. Although Zionist interest in crusader material culture had a late beginning, the fact that they were prominent elements in the country's physical and cultural landscape, and that some were located in the midst of areas of Zionist colonisation, meant that they could not be ignored. Material culture found at the site was used to impart central Zionist ideological concepts.

Subsequent changes related to the castle and its surroundings carried with it yet a different perception of the crusader castle in Zionist writing. From the 1920s the British Mandatory Government of Palestine restricted Jewish immigration into Palestine, and in the 1930s fixed a quota of immigration certificates. With the reduction of certificates and the deteriorating situation in Europe, the number of illegal immigrants rose drastically. This led to the creation in the summer of 1939 of a temporary detention camp in 'Athlit, built at a short distance to the north of the Templar castle. Although the castle and the detention camp were two separate sites a few kilometres apart, in popular perception 'Athlit would be from now on better known due to this camp.[35] The detention camp operated until the creation of the State of Israel in 1948, and it is interesting to see how the history of the Templar castle and the camp were interconnected in Zionist popular writing. Two newspaper articles by Meysels, published in the *Palestine Post* in 1941, highlight this point. In an article titled 'A Modern Castellum Peregrinorum. Refugee's Life at 'Athlit' published in January 1941, Meysels described in great detail the life of the Jewish refugees interned in 'Athlit detention camp. Relevant for our purposes in trying to understand the changing Zionist perception of a crusader castle, is the article's beginning. In the first two paragraphs Meysels gives a short historical survey of the site, making a clear analogy between the thirteenth-century castle and the twentieth-century detention camp.[36] He wrote that the castle was built by, 'the Templars who performed something like police duties at the time of the Frankish Kingdom and was used by them as an immense "Castellum Peregrinorum"'. He went on to describe the castle in which the pilgrims might shelter, but then added 'here the thousands, who came to the Holy Land as pilgrims were interrogated and examined before being allowed to join the caravan that started out from Acre.' Meysels made an analogy between the pilgrims of the past and the contemporary refuges, all in search of the promised land. Himself a refugee, who fled Vienna in 1938 and arrived in Palestine as a tourist to only later acquire legal immigration status,[37] he called refuges from Rumania interned at 'Athlit, 'pilgrims in search of a home'. For Meysels the detention camp of the present, where these Rumanian and other Jewish refugees were incarcerated, was simultaneously the castle of the past, and he drew a distinct parallel between these two sites: 'Today three small watch towers mark the site of 'Athlit's new pilgrims' castle, whose modern name is "Clearance Camp" [...] which is surrounded by a low fence of barbed wire.'[38]

Meysels was in awe of the size, strength, and architectural sophistication of the Templar castle, and in another article titled 'The Pilgrims' Castle', published in the *Palestine Post* a month later, he went into great detail describing the castle's different halls, which were well-fitted for the pilgrims who had to spend their first weeks in the Holy Land under 'strict supervision'. Meysels describes 'Athlit as, 'a perfect specimen of the medieval fortress'. Like Ben Zvi, Meysels placed the castle's origins in the country's Jewish past. 'It would be wholly erroneous to assume that the Crusaders had brought the highly developed stone-mason's technique with them from Europe. They learned this art from the ancient Romans and above all', he stressed, 'from the builders of the ancient Jewish fortresses in the country [...]'.[39] Meysels' nationalistic interpretation of 'Athlit is instructive. At a time when crusader architecture and physical remains were being used by European historians to construct nationalist identities, Meysels emphasised the Jewish heritage of this imposing crusader castle.

In this article Meysels developed further the analogy between the castle and the detention camp. He wrote that on the road from Tel Aviv to Haifa one encounters and admires the 'heroic silhouette of the Pilgrims' Castle at 'Athlit [...] which has taken us back to the Middle Ages, into the ironclad period of the Crusaders' Kingdom, so remote in time yet furnishing such surprisingly close parallels to the present.' According to Meysels this similarity was also revealed in the excavations undertaken by the Department of Antiquities from 1930, from which one 'conjured up a vivid picture of the conglomeration of stone houses, the first home of the poor newcomers to the Palestine of the 13th century. Here they were interrogated, medically examined and, according to their country of origin, assigned to one or other of the relief organizations, unless it was their fate to be shipped hack again'.

Conclusion

Changing patterns of perception and interpretation of the Crusader castle of 'Athlit by Zionist writers, at the beginning of the twentieth century, show its use to impart Zionist ideals, such as an historical continuity between the Jewish past and the Zionist national revival. Meysels' analogy between the Crusader castle of 'Athlit and the detention camp of the 1940s, shows also its uses to reflect upon the castle's role in the contemporary Jewish history and in the fate of the many other homeless and vulnerable refugees fleeing Europe. For Meysels – a persecuted refugee – the only purpose of the castle during the Frankish period was, as in his time, to serve as a camp for immigrants, many of them illegal. 'The "tourist traffic" of the Frankish Kingdom was not confined to the legitimate participants of the large-scale and "official" crusades.' Meysels wrote, 'Apart from these "certificate holders", many thousands entered the country annually [...]'. It ['Athlit] acted as a kind of Immigration Department for crusaders not under the protection of a sovereign or feudal lord. [...] The name was meant to denote that it served as a quarantine station, a clearance camp for pilgrims. There is nothing new under the sun, even at 'Athlit.[40]

Notes

1. Theodor F. Meysels, 'The Pilgrim's Castle', *Palestine Post* vol. XV, no. 4491, 16 February 1941, p. 6.
2. On the Palestine Post see 'The Palestine Post', *The National Library Newspaper Collection, The National Library of Israel*, <https://www.nli.org.il/en/newspapers/pls>, [accessed 24 March 2022].
3. For the role of material culture in the shaping of a national identity in Israel see, for example, M. Feige, 'Introduction', in *Archaeology and Nationalism in Eretz-Israel*, eds. M. Feige and Z. Shiloni (Jerusalem, 2008), pp. 3–7 [Hebrew]; N. Silberman, and D. Small, eds., *The Archaeology of Israel* (Sheffield, 1997); Y. Zerubavel, *Recovered Roots* (Chicago, IL, 1995); N. Abu el-Haj, *Facts on the Ground* (Chicago, IL, 2001); R. Kletter, *Just Past? The Making of Israeli Archaeology* (London, 2006); J. Bronstein, 'Zionism, Medieval Culture, and National Discourse', *Memoirs of the American Academy in Rome* 62 (2017), pp. 119–35.
4. For recent studies on the thirteenth-century crusader castle see articles by Helen Nicholson, Vardit Shoten-Hallel, Yvonne Friedman and Yves Gleize, published in G. Fishhof, J. Bronstein and V. Shotten-Hallel (eds.), *Settlement and Crusade in the Thirteenth Century: Multidisciplinary Studies of the Latin East, Crusades – Subsidia* (Abingdon, 2021). For an example of a nineteenth century perception of the castle, see an 1874 description by Claude Conder, who wrote that, judging from its impressive remains, 'Athlit must have been the finest town of the crusader period in the country. Charles Clermont-Ganneau, 'The Survey of Palestine' (London, 1874), p. 13.
5. On these colonies see, for example, Y. Ben-Arieh, *The Making of Eretz Israel in the Modern Era* (Berlin, 2020), pp. 213–69.
6. J. Bronstein, 'Reviving Forgotten Jewish Heroes: An Aspect of Early 20th Century Zionist Perception of the Crusader Period in Palestine', *Jewish Quarterly Review* 109 (2019), pp. 634–36.
7. See for example, B.Z. Kedar, 'Il motivo della crociata nel pensiero politico israeliano', in *Verso Gerusalemme. II Convegno Internazionale nel IX Centenario della I Crociata (1099–1999). Bari, 11–13 gennaio 1999*, eds. F. Cardini, M. Belloli and B. Vetere (Lecce: Congedo, 1999), pp. 135–50; B.Z. Kedar, 'Joshua Prawer (1917–1990), Historian of the Crusading Kingdom of Jerusalem', *Mediterranean Historical Review* 5 (1990), pp. 107–16; R. Ellenblum, *Crusader Castles and Modern Histories* (Cambridge, 2007), pp. 57–61. On the analogy's political uses see also D. Ohana, *The Origins of Israeli Mythology* (Cambridge, 2012), pp. 131–82.
8. Ibid., p. 143

9   Kalman Shlomo Kantor, 'Mikhtav le-Arye Leib Horowitz [Letter to Arye Leib Horowitz]', *Ha Melitz* 113, 7 June 1888, col. 1196; J. Bronstein, 'Early Zionists and Crusader Castles: Perceptions and Interpretations of Crusader Material Culture in the Late Nineteenth and the Early Twentieth Centuries', *Jewish Culture and History* 20 (2019), pp. 337–58.
10 On Haim Hissin see Shulamit Laskov's introduction to a compilation of his articles in H. Hissin, *Masa'ba-Erets ha-mubtahat* [A Journey to the Promised Land], trans. H. Ben-Amram; Introduction and notes S. Laskov (Tel-Aviv: Hakibbutz Hameuchad, 1982), pp. 7–15 [Hebrew].
11 Ibid., pp. 336–37, 343–45; Bronstein, 'Early Zionists', pp. 346–48.
12 Hissin, *Masa'ba-Erets,* p. 346; my translation.
13 Ibid.
14 Ibid.
15 'Baron James Rothschild in Zichron Ya'akov', *Doar Hayom*, 7 April 1921, p. 3 [Hebrew].
16 Y. Harari, *Bein ha-Kramim* [Amongst the Vineyards] (Tel-Aviv, 1947), p. 129 [Hebrew]; Bronstein, 'Early Zionists', p. 341.
17 Y. Erez (ed.), *Sefer ha-Alyia ha-shlishit* [The Book of the Third Aliyah], vol. 1 (Tel Aviv, 1964), p. 224 [Hebrew]. At times the castle of 'Athlit was not only an historical place to visit or view from afar, but also a place to live. A letter sent by a woman pioneer in 'Athlit in *c.*1921 referred to a small group of five fishermen, demobilized from the Jewish Legion of North America volunteers, who settled in the ruins of the castle and developed the fishing industry there (an enterprise that lasted only for two years). See letter by Sarah bat-Hilel Yenovsky, 'Hachara haklait' [Agricultural Training], in Erez (ed.) *Sefer ha-Alyia ha-shlishit,* p. 757.
18 T. ben-Yosef, *Yed'iat ha'arets ke thum hinuhi ba-tarbut ha-Zionist le-'or hitpathuto ba, 'afik ha-'amami be-shnot 1921–1973* [Yediyat ha-aretz (learning the land of Israel) as an educational field in Zionist culture], Ph.D. dissertation, University of Tel Aviv, 2003, p. 13 [Hebrew].
19 Y. Ben-Arieh, 'Development in the Study of Yediat ha-Aretz in Modern Times, up to the Establishment of the State of Israel', *Cathedra* 100 (2001), pp. 306–38 [Hebrew]; S. Katz, 'The Israeli Teacher Guide: The Emergence and Perpetuation of a Role', *Annals of Tourism Research* 12 (1985), pp. 57–59; S. Fine, *Art and Judaism in the Greco-Roman World: Towards a New Jewish Archaeology* (Cambridge, 2005), pp. 22–23; Bronstein, 'Zionism', pp. 121–23.
20 He also referred to the establishment in 'Athlit of the agricultural experimental station, see Y. Press, *Erets Ysra'el ve-Suria ha-dromit, sefer masa'ot* [Palestine and South-Syria, a Book of Travels] (Jerusalem, 1921), pp. 268–69 [Hebrew].
21 A.J. Brawer, *Haaretz*: sefer li-yedi'at Erets Yisra'el [The Land of Israel: A Book for knowing/learning the Land] (Tel Aviv: Dvir, 1928), pp. 164–65, 238 [Hebrew].
22 Ibid. p. 316.
23 Ellenblum, *Crusader Castles*, pp. 64–68.
24 Elizabeth Siberry, 'Images of the Crusades in the Nineteenth and Twentieth Centuries', *in The Oxford Illustrated History of the Crusades*, ed. J. Riley-Smith (Oxford, 1995), pp. 385–89; Siberry, *New Crusaders.*
25 Horswell, *British Crusader Medievalism*, p. 149.

26 'In connection with the preparation of a list of names of Palestinian villages, required for the census of November 1922, our board, with government approval, chose from among its members a committee to determine the historical Hebrew names of these villages'. *Proceedings of the Jewish Palestine Exploration Society. Being an Abridgment of the Hebrew Kovets ha-hevrah ha-'Ivrit le-hakirat Erets Yisra`el ve-'Atikoteah* (Jerusalem, 1925), p. 89. On the importance of the identification, location, and concretisation of names of places of historical significance for the Zionist process of nation building see Yaakov Shavit, 'Emet me-Erets Titsmah,' Kavim le-hitpathut ha-'inian ha-tsiburi be-`arkeologiah (`ad shnot ha-shloshim)' ['Truth should Spring out of the Earth: The Development of Jewish Popular Interest in Archaeology in Eretz Israel], *Cathedra* 44 (1987), p. 47 [Hebrew].

27 On the activities of the Society from 1920 to 1925, see Y. Press, 'Report on the work of the Jewish Exploration Society', *Proceedings of the Jewish Palestine Exploration Society. Being an Abridgment of the Hebrew Kovets ha-hevrah ha-'Ivrit le-hakirat Erets Yisra`el ve-'Atikoteah* (Jerusalem: Jewish Palestine exploration society, 1925, p, 90; *Kovets ha-hevrah ha-'Ivrit le-hakirat Erets Yisra`el ve-'Atikoteah*, ed. N. Slouchz (Tel Aviv, 1921).

28 Principally, the first archaeological excavation conducted by Nahum Slouschz on behalf of the Jewish Palestinian Excavation Society, in 1921 in Hammat Tiberias, Tiberia's hot springs, at the southern borders of ancient city of Tiberias, see Bronstein, 'Zionism'.

29 Y. Ben Zvi, ''Athlit, shma ve-'atikoteah'[Athlit, its name and Ancient Remains'], *Kovets ha-hevrah ha-'Ivrit le-hakirat `Erets Yisra`el ve-'Atikoteah*, ed. N. Slouchz (Tel Aviv, 1921), p. 111.

30 Although Ben Zvi explained that it was difficult to establish the origin of the name 'Athlit, he concluded by examining these two artefacts as well as by an etymological and historical discussion, that 'Athlit was an ancient Hebrew name, deriving from the biblical 'Atali' or 'Athalia'. These were probably the first letters of the most familiar name Athaliah, wife of King Jehoram, queen consort, and for a short period queen regnant of Judah in the ninth century BC. Ben Zvi, ''Athlit, shma ve-'atikoteah', pp. 112–13.

31 'Be mahtsevot Athlit' ['In 'Athlit's Quarries'], *Davar,* 6 November1931, p. 8.

32 Y. Ben Zvi, *Shaar Yeshuv: maamarim u prakim be divrei ha yeshuv ha Hivri ve Eretz Israel u ve heker ha moledet* [Remnants of Ancient Hebrew Communities in the Land of Israel: Articles and Chapters in the History of the Hebrew Communities in the Land of Israel and in the Study of the Homeland] (Tel Aviv, 1927), pp. 132–37; G. Shimoni, *The Zionist Ideology* (Hannover, 1997), pp. 351–61; Bronstein, 'Zionism'.

33 Ben Zvi, 'Athlit, shma ve-'atikoteah', pp. 112–13.

34 See Ben-Zvi, *Sha'ar Yeshuv*, p. 4; On the concept of 'redeeming the Land' see B. Neumann, *Land and Desire in Early Zionism*, trans. H. Watzman (Waltham, MA, 2011), pp. 80–81.

35 Walter Laqueur, *A History of Zionism* (New York, 2009; first edition 1972), pp. 528–31; A.J. Kochavi, 'The Struggle against Jewish Immigration to Palestine', *Middle Eastern Studies* 34 (1998), pp. 146–67. The

'Athlit Detention Camp, is today a National Heritage Site, and serves a museum and educational centre; see 'Atlit Detention Camp', *The Council for Conservation of Heritage Sites in Israel*, <https://shimur.org/sites/atlit-detention-camp/?lang=en>, [accessed 24 March 2022].
36 Theodor F. Meysels, 'A Modern Castellum Peregrinorum. Refugee's Life at 'Athlit', *Palestine Post*, vol. XV, no. 4464, 15 January 1941, p. 4.
37 On Theodor F. Meysels see Werner Röder and Herbert A. Strauss (eds.) *Biographisches Handbuch der deutschsprachigen Emigration nach 1933–1945*, Institut für Zeitgeschichte and Research Foundation for Jewish Immigration (Berlin, 2016), p. 815.
38 Meysels, 'A Modern Castellum Peregrinorum', p. 4.
39 Meysels, 'The Pilgrim's Castle', p. 6.
40 Ibid.

Bibliography

Primary

'Atlit Detention Camp'. *The Council for Conservation of Heritage Sites in Israel*, https://shimur.org/sites/atlit-detention-camp/?lang=en. Accessed 24 March 2022.
'Baron James Rothschild in Zichron Ya'akov', *Doar Hayom*, 07.04.1921, p. 3 [Hebrew].
'Be mahtsevot Athlit' ['In 'Athlit's Quarries']. *Davar* 06.11.1931, p. 8 [Hebrew].
Ben Zvi, Y. "Athlit, shma ve-'atikoteah'[Athlit, its name and Ancient Remains']. In *Kovets 'ha-hevrah ha-'Ivrit le-hakirat `Erets Yisra`el ve-'Atikoteah*. Ed. N. Slouchz. Tel Aviv: unknown publisher, 1921, pp. 111–17 [Hebrew].
———. *Shaar Yeshuv: maamarim u prakim be divrei ha yeshuv ha Hivri ve Eretz Israel u ve heker ha moledet* [Remnants of Ancient Hebrew Communities in the Land of Israel: Articles and Chapters in the History of the Hebrew Communities in the Land of Israel and in the Study of the Homeland]. Tel Aviv: Davar, 1927.
Brawer, A.J. *Haaretz: sefer li-yedi'at Erets Yisra'el* [The Land of Israel: A Book for knowing/learning the Land]. Tel Aviv: Dvir, 1928 [Hebrew].
Clermont-Ganneau, Charles. '*The Survey of Palestine*'. London: Palestine Exploration Fund, 1874.
Erez, Y. ed. *Sefer ha-Alyia ha-shlishit* [The Book of the Third Aliyah]. Vol. 1. Tel Aviv: 'Am 'Oved, 1964 [Hebrew].
Harari, Y. *Bein ha-Kramim* [Amongst the Vineyards]. Tel-Aviv: Dvir, 1947 [Hebrew].
Kantor, Kalman Shlomo. 'Mikhtav le-Arye Leib Horowitz [Letter to Arye Leib Horowitz]'. *Ha Melitz* 113, 7 June 1888, col. 1196.
Meysels, Theodor F. 'A Modern Castellum Peregrinorum. Refugee's Life at 'Athlit'. *Palestine Post*. Vol. XV, no. 4464. 15 January 1941, p. 4.
———. 'The Pilgrim's Castle'. *Palestine Post*. Vol. XV, no. 4491. 16 February 1941, p. 6.

Press, Y. *Erets Ysra'el ve-Suria ha-dromit, sefer masa'ot* [Palestine and South-Syria, a Book of Travels]. Jerusalem: Harz, 1921 [Hebrew].

———. 'Report on the work of the Jewish Exploration Society'. *Proceedings of the Jewish Palestine Exploration Society. Being an Abridgment of the Hebrew Kovets ha-hevrah ha-'Ivrit le-hakirat Erets Yisra`el ve-'Atikoteah*. Jerusalem: Jewish Palestine Exploration Society, 1925, pp. 91–94.

Slouchz, N. ed. *Kovets ha-hevrah ha-'Ivrit le-hakirat Erets Yisra`el ve-'Atikoteah*. Tel Aviv: Dfus A. Eitan and S. Shoshani, 1921.

Secondary

Abu el-Haj, N. *Facts on the Ground: Archaeological Practice and Territorial Self-Fashioning in Israeli Society*. Chicago, IL: University of Chicago Press, 2001.

Ben-Arieh, Y. 'Development in the Study of Yediat ha-Aretz in Modern Times, up to the Establishment of the State of Israel'. *Cathedra* 100 (2001), pp. 306–38 [Hebrew].

———. *The Making of Eretz Israel in the Modern Era: A Historical-Geographical Study (1799–1949)*. Berlin: De Gruyter Oldenbourg, 2020.

Ben-Yosef, T. *Yed'iat ha'arets ke thum hinuhi ba-tarbut ha-Zionist le-`or hit-pathuto ba, `afik ha-`amami be-shnot 1921–1973* [Learning the land of Israel as an educational field in Zionist culture]. Ph.D. Dissertation. University of Tel Aviv, 2003 [Hebrew].

Bronstein, Judith. 'Zionism, Medieval Culture, and National Discourse'. *Memoirs of the American Academy in Rome* 62 (2017), pp. 119–35.

———. 'Early Zionists and Crusader Castles: Perceptions and Interpretations of Crusader Material Culture in the Late Nineteenth and the Early Twentieth Centuries'. *Jewish Culture and History* 20 (2019), pp. 337–58.

———. 'Reviving Forgotten Jewish Heroes: An Aspect of Early 20th Century Zionist Perception of the Crusader Period in Palestine'. *Jewish Quarterly Review* 109 (2019), pp. 634–36.

Ellenblum, R. *Crusader Castles and Modern Histories*. Cambridge: Cambridge University Press, 2007.

Feige, M. 'Introduction'. In *Archaeology and Nationalism in Eretz-Israel*. Eds. M. Feige and Z. Shiloni. Jerusalem: Ben-Gurion Research Institute, 2008, pp. 3–7 [Hebrew].

Fine, S. *Art and Judaism in the Greco-Roman World: Towards a New Jewish Archaeology*. Cambridge: Cambridge University Press, 2005.

Fishhof, G., J. Bronstein and V. Shotten-Hallel, eds. *Settlement and Crusade in the Thirteenth Century: Multidisciplinary Studies of the Latin East, Crusades – Subsidia*. Abingdon: Routledge, 2021.

Hissin, H. *Masa' ba-Erets ha-mubtahat* [A Journey to the Promised Land]. Ed. S. Laskov. Trans. H. Ben-Amram. Tel-Aviv: Hakibbutz Hameuchad, 1982 [Hebrew].

Horswell, Mike. *The Rise and Fall of British Crusader Medievalism, c. 1825–1945*. Abingdon: Routledge, 2018.

Katz, S. 'The Israeli Teacher Guide: The Emergence and Perpetuation of a Role'. *Annals of Tourism Research* 12 (1985), pp. 57–59.

Kedar, B.Z. 'Joshua Prawer (1917–1990), Historian of the Crusading Kingdom of Jerusalem'. *Mediterranean Historical Review* 5 (1990), pp. 107–16.

———. 'Il motivo della crociata nel pensiero politico israeliano'. In *Verso Gerusalemme. II Convegno Internazionale nel IX Centenario della I Crociata (1099–1999). Bari, 11–13 gennaio 1999*. Eds. F. Cardini, M. Belloli and B. Vetere. Lecce: Congedo, 1999, pp. 135–50.

Kletter, R. *Just Past? The Making of Israeli Archaeology*. London: Equinox, 2006.

Kochavi, A.J. 'The Struggle against Jewish Immigration to Palestine'. *Middle Eastern Studies* 34 (1998), pp. 146–67.

Laqueur, Walter. *A History of Zionism: From the French Revolution to the Establishment of the State of Israel*. New York: Schocken Books, 2009 (first edn. 1972).

Neumann, B. *Land and Desire in Early Zionism*. Trans. H. Watzman. Waltham, MA: Brandeis University Press, 2011.

Ohana, D. *The Origins of Israeli Mythology: Neither Canaanites nor Crusaders*. Cambridge: Cambridge University Press, 2012.

Röder, Werner, and Herbert A. Strauss eds. *Biographisches Handbuch der deutschsprachigen Emigration nach 1933–1945*. Institut für Zeitgeschichte and Research Foundation for Jewish Immigration. Berlin: K.G. Saur, 2016.

Shavit, Yaakov. 'Emet me-Erets Titsmah,' Kavim le-hitpathut ha-'inian ha-tsiburi be-'arkeologiah ('ad shnot ha-shloshim)' [Truth should Spring out of the Earth: The Development of Jewish Popular Interest in Archaeology in Eretz Israel]. *Cathedra* 44 (1987), pp. 27–54 [Hebrew].

Shimoni, G. *The Zionist Ideology*. Hannover: Brandeis University Press, 1997.

Siberry, Elizabeth. 'Images of the Crusades in the Nineteenth and Twentieth Centuries'. In *The Oxford Illustrated History of the Crusades*. Ed. J. Riley-Smith. Oxford: OUP, 1995, pp. 385–89.

———. *The New Crusaders. Images of the Crusades in the 19th and Early 20th Centuries*. Aldershot: Ashgate, 2000.

Silberman, N. and D. Small, eds. *The Archaeology of Israel: Constructing the Past, Interpreting the Present*. Sheffield: Sheffield Academic Press, 1997.

'The Palestine Post'. *The National Library Newspaper Collection. The National Library of Israel*. https://www.nli.org.il/en/newspapers/pls. Accessed 24 March 2022.

Zerubavel, Y. *Recovered Roots: Collective Memory and the Making of Israeli National Tradition*. Chicago, IL: University of Chicago Press, 1995.

4 Cultural Brokers in the Nationalisation of Crusader Architecture

Astrid Swenson

Introduction: agency in the nationalisation of the crusades

This chapter discusses how attention to 'cultural brokers' can help to understand the modern nationalisation of the crusades as a transcultural process by directing the gaze to the complex human interactions which shaped the interest in, and transformation of, crusader architecture in the Mediterranean in the first half of the twentieth century.[1] As testified by other chapters across this volume, the rich literature on the reception of the crusades[2] is becoming increasingly interested in materiality.[3] The modern colonisation of the Mediterranean by different European powers opened the door not just for historiographic explorations but for national acquisitions, restorations, and transformations of crusader sites. Following a blood-and-soil logic of nationalism, the presence of crusader vestiges (a term that was often used loosely and generally included the Hospitallers and, when convenient, also encompassed other 'Latin' remains from the Normans to the Venetians) helped to stake claims that territories once conquered by crusaders should return home 'again'.

In a region of competing imperial claims, sites connected to the history of the crusades therefore attracted the attention of all the major European powers. While the French, British, and Italians established formal empires in the Mediterranean, other European interest in these sites was also strong. For each nation, interventions for restoration or acquisition were not limited to territories under their own rule, but extended into Ottoman territories, post-independence Greece, as well as the other European empires. These cross-cutting linkages allow us to use the crusader sites as a prism for comparing formal and informal imperial heritage policies and for tracing the interdependencies between them. While imperial actors frequently claimed that the Latinness of the crusader remains made the West the only interested party, these sites – which

DOI: 10.4324/9781003241935-5

were part of the rural, urban, and religious fabric of different communities – also interested others. Local and diasporic Maltese, Greek, Turkish, Arab, and Jewish actors, for instance, had their own agendas for the use, preservation, or destruction of sites, as did transnational bodies, especially the various successor organisations to the Knights of St. John and later the League of Nations and the United Nations.

The crusader vestiges are particularly intriguing as they represent a unique category between a heritage of the self and a heritage of the other across time. Sites of conflict and encounter in the past as well as the present, and altered by various conquerors and inhabitants over the centuries, they could be claimed by a multitude of heirs. Hence, the architectural fabric of remains was used to negotiate and display evolving relations between different groups.

The cross-cultural processes that were operating, are neither simply transnational or imperial, nor limited to the Mediterranean. To understand them it is useful to pay attention to what Jane Kaplan in a different context called 'the microhistory of geopolitics'.[4] As a result, I am interested not just in the representation of sites, but also in their intimate histories and transculturations. Who were the people who turned sites into national monuments? How did they relate to the site? And how did their interventions change the relationship other people had with them, from local inhabitants, prisoners forced to do the building work, soldiers sent there during conflict and leave, to ever increasing numbers of tourists? Relating these intimate appropriations to the colonial discourses about the buildings pronounced in the metropole can, I argue, help us to think in a more nuanced way about agency and the role of tangible and intangible 'spaces in between'.

In this chapter, I will discuss how attention to what are referred to variously as 'cultural brokers', 'intermediaries', and 'go-betweens', might help to better understand the emergence, and enduring relevance, of the nationalisation of the crusades. The literature on the medieval and early modern crusades has increasingly been concerned with the nature of encounter and has brought together crusade history with the anthropological literature on encounters.[5] Intermediaries are also present in the growing literature on the modern memory of the crusades as well as in the literature on particular sites, but their role remains under-theorised, and their lives could be more systematically compared and connected.[6]

The notions of 'cultural brokers', 'intermediaries', and 'go-betweens' was primarily developed for zones of new contact in the early modern period, rather than for an area like the Mediterranean with its millennia of encounters.[7] But the idea is useful to conceptualise agency amidst the transnational, transcultural, and global forces that have shaped processes of memorialisation and heritagisation more broadly.[8] Recent years have seen a shift in studies of Middle Eastern archaeology highlighting interactions and non-western agency,[9] which complicate the often relatively abstract notions of agency in critiques of the nationalisation of heritage in critical heritage studies.[10]

I am using the notion of 'cultural brokers', 'intermediaries', and 'go-betweens' loosely to indicate various levels of influence and visibility, locating the lives of different intermediaries in place and space, directing the gaze 'on the ground' to some of a much wider range of human relations that underpinned the acquisition, restoration, and transformation of crusader sites across the Mediterranean in the early twentieth century. Broader tensions between nationalism and internationalism will be discussed through brief spotlights on three buildings and their brokers, revealing the importance of different political contexts, but also the role of personal relationships across borders of culture, status, and power. First, the correspondence between the directors of the German and Italian Archaeological Institutes in Athens, Georg Karo and Luigi Pernier, about the archaeological remains at Lindos on the Island of Rhodes will set the scene for discussing how the Italian annexation of the Dodecanes in 1912 unsettled the international sphere and accelerated the nationalisation of crusader sites. Second, the celebration of the addition of a minaret to the former Lusignan Cathedral at Famagusta as a sign of cultural cooperation at a time of increasing ethnic and national tension in interwar Cyprus will be unpacked through the relationship between Cyprus' first Curator of Ancient Monuments, George Jeffery, and the delegate of the Evcaf, in charge of Muslim buildings, Munir Bey. Finally, the interactions of Parisian museum director Paul Deschamps and the Guardian of the Crac des Chevaliers in Syria, Assad Abbas, in the 1930s and 1940s will address issues of displacement and silencing of indigenous voices. The chapter will compare these intermediaries and situate them in wider sets of contacts to consider agency and limits of power in the nationalisation of the crusades.

Relationships and the politics of emotions

The first vignette takes place in the context of the Italian annexation of the Dodecanese which accelerated the nationalisation of crusader sites internationally. Set in Athens in 1912, the episode is also a reminder of the networks of scholarly friendships which shaped the field of crusader studies before, during, and after the age of nationalism.

'Dear friend, the Minister of Public Instruction forwarded me your letter to the General Directorate of Fine Arts about the Danish excavation at Lindos asking for urgent explanations [...] Given the friendship you always had for me, it hurts me that you did not warn me or ask me for advice before listening to such rumours',[11] wrote a wounded Luigi Pernier, director of the recently created Italian Archaeological School of Athens in the summer of 1913 to Georg Karo, his counterpart at the German Archaeological Institute in the Greek capital. Pernier (1874–1937) was an Italian archaeologist best known for his discovery of the Disc of Phaistos. Following work as inspector of museums, galleries, and excavations of antiquities in Florence and with the Italian Mission to Crete, he was appointed in 1909 as the first director of the newly established Italian Archaeological School of Athens.[12] Karo (1872–1963) worked on the influence of 'oriental' cultures on Greek and Etruscan art and on Minoan and Mycenaean culture. He joined the Deutsches Archäologisches Institut (DAI) in Athens in 1905 as secretary and from 1910 to 1919 was 'first director'. The two men not only shared a similar professional role in the same city but also were of the same age and spoke to each other in Italian as Karo had spent his childhood in Florence before embarking on his academic career in Germany.[13]

The Italian annexation of the Dodecanese during the Italian-Turkish war in 1912, however, unsettled their friendship, and the international archaeological sphere more broadly. Members of foreign archaeological missions who had been working on the islands until the occupation soon complained about the treatment of antiquities. The Danish mission denounced the destruction and dispersal carried out by Italian soldiers in the area around Lindos on Rhodes, where hundreds of fragments preserved in a little museum built at the turn of the century were devastated because of the war.[14]

As the Danish archaeologists were working in Rhodes under the protection of the German Embassy of Constantinople, Georg Karo felt compelled to mediate. In a letter to the Italian authorities, Karo pointed out that the director of the Italian Archaeological school in Athens had promised during the recent international Archaeological Congress in Rome that an international commission would be created to protect the interests of all foreigners working in the occupied territories; but now it seemed this promise had been violated. A protest was started in Berlin. Karo asked for reassurance that rumours about spoliation were untrue, as these would harm the reputation of Italian science.

Given their friendship, why did Karo choose not to use his personal relation to Pernier? He certainly had thought about it. As Karo explained to his *'carissimo'* upon receiving his distressed missive, the German archaeologist even had even sought his mother's advice about the disturbing affair. Yet it was precisely because of their friendship that he had decided in the end not to write to Pernier directly. He had not wanted to bother his dearest friend as he never for a second suspected him – or any Italian archaeologist for the matter. On the contrary, Karo appeared entirely convinced the military was to blame. Regretting the diplomatic entanglements, he now very much hoped that the whole business would be over soon. A few angry letters between Karo and the Italian military leadership followed (respectively blaming Italian troops and German professors to be the looters) but before the case could be 'blown into an international episode, resulting in the breaking off of diplomatic relations', the loss of objects was conveniently blamed on 'Turkish gendarmes'. The Danes and the international community were satisfied with the explanation,[15] and a reconciled Pernier and Karo resumed discussing scholarly matters. They shared their excitement about the possibilities that the Italian annexation brought for the planned restorations of Rhodes' crusader (i.e., Hospitaller) sites as symbols of the island's longstanding Westernness.[16]

The Italian occupation in the Aegean set in motion several programmes for the nationalisation of the Latin monuments of the islands, and accelerated the appropriation of crusader sites elsewhere. Although Italy had agreed to return the Dodecanese to the Ottoman Empire in the Treaty of Ouchy in 1912, the provisional Italian administration remained on the island, and a programme of architectural Italianisation began almost immediately. On the 'Street of Knights' in Rhodes, which housed the Inns or 'Auberges' of the different 'Languages' of the Order of St. John, the Italian restorations removed most transformations that had occurred during the Ottoman Period. The uses of the Hospitaller past for proving the long-standing *Italianità* of the region were enhanced after the formal annexation by Fascist Italy in 1923, most spectacularly through the rebuilding of the Palace of the Grand Masters in Rhodes in the late 1930s.[17] Vittorio Emmanuele III and Benito Mussolini are still remembered by a massive marble plaque at the entrance.

However, the nationalisations were not limited to the Italians. In 1910, the French consul at Rhodes, Adalbert Laffon had already written to Maurice Bompard, ambassador of France in Constantinople, with ideas to restore the Auberge de France on the Street of the Knights. Bompard used the chaos of the Italo-Turkish war to acquire the building and gift it to France. He too remains to this day remembered by a (slightly smaller) marble plaque stating 'Mr Bompard, French Ambassador in Constantinople, gifted this building to the State. This witness to the glory of France in the East was acquired by him and restored by Mr Gabriel, architect, Mr Laffon being consul in Rhodes in 1913.'[18] Two years later the Auberge was listed on the French National Monument Register. Other sites from the crusader period, most famously the Crac des Chevaliers in Syria, would soon be inscribed as part of as a small number of properties outside metropolitan France.

While the British State generally had much less inclination than its French counterpart to spend money on heritage sites inside or outside of the British Isles, it often used intermediaries with strong links to the state, such as the Venerable Order of St. John. Hence, the British Delegation at the 1919 Peace Conference, who expressed the hope that the Italians rather than the Greeks might retain the island, were in favour that the Grand Priory of England would acquire the 'Auberge d'Angleterre', so that this heritage could be preserved for the nation.[19]

At Lindos, with whose antiquities this chapter began, the visual record of the transformations of the remains left by the Hospitallers is also apparent, but the twenty-first century narrative tells visitors little about the entanglements that underpinned the restorations in the interwar period. Rather, the narrative on the signs testifies to a process of Greek nationalisation by focussing on the need to 'de-restore' Italian additions of ancient sites for reasons of quality and durability.

Given their specialisms in earlier periods and subsequent changes of workplace Karo and Pernier were peripheral rather than central to the unfolding restorations of crusader sites (Pernier was made director of the Archaeological Museum of Florence giving up his directorship of the Athens school in 1914 while Karo left Athens for a professorship in Halle in 1920. He returned to Athens as the director of the DAI but was dismissed in 1936 because of his Jewish family background. He then emigrated to the United States in 1939, returning to Freiburg in 1953 for the last ten years of his life). However, their institutions in Athens remained important actors throughout the troubled first half of the twentieth century. Moreover, their correspondence in the files of the Central State Archive in Rome appears interesting for the purpose of this book not least as it reminds us how deeply the burgeoning archaeological and architectural interest in the crusades enmeshed with the broader archaeological sphere and the politics of the past, and by drawing attention to the role of 'third spaces' (far from the actual 'contact zones') like Athens with its concentration of foreign institutes. The mixture of nationalism and internationalism underlying Karo and Pernier's interactions, but also the fragility of the international 'middle ground' the actors operated in, and the construction of this international scholarly sphere through the othering of 'Orientals' as uncivilised

82 *Astrid Swenson*

'vandals' in a colonial context (familiar tropes in the history of classical archaeology) would remain recurrent themes in the history of the modern nationalisation of the architecture of the crusades.

What appears perhaps even more interesting is the multitude of overlapping intermediary roles each protagonist had to adopt: between and within national politics; among scholarly communities; and negotiating the international world of itinerant congresses, local international institutes and 'on site' preservationist work. These roles enmeshed with their private lives and sometimes resulted in attempts to dissociate one's different personas. As a result, the exchange of letters between Pernier and Karo (and their constant forwarding across Europe as both archaeologists were travelling at the time in third countries) points not so much to the existence of one 'space in between' in which the nationalisation of even a single crusader site was negotiated but of many overlapping ones.

Building third spaces

These overlapping spheres are also apparent when we move the gaze to our two other case studies and their brokers: the Cathedral-Mosque of Famagusta and the Crac des Chevaliers in Syria. Both underwent substantial restoration in the 1930s. To the first a minaret was added under the auspices of the 'Evcaf' – the Muslim Board of Turkish Commissioners for Charitable and Religious Purposes in Cyprus – in collaboration with the Island's first Conservator for Ancient Monuments, George Everett Jeffery. The architect of St. George's Anglican Cathedral and College in Jerusalem had worked as an Inspector of Public Works in Cyprus in 1899–1900 and then (with a short intermission after the First World War) as Curator of Ancient Monuments he was virtually the only Englishmen in the colonial administration in charge of Cyprus' historic monuments for 35 years.[20] About the restoration and his collaboration with the Evcaf, Jeffery wrote in an official report:

> The new minaret at Famagusta may perhaps be regarded as onemore [sic] link in that series of monuments which recalls the amicable relations between Christians and Moslems before and during the earlier Crusades – Charlemagne and his friend Haroun er Rashid, Frederick II in the Mosque of Omar, not forgetting the romance of Coeur de Lion and Salah e'Din, or the fact that in the Holy City of Jerusalem most of the more important shrines are still common to both religions as they have been ever since the era of the Hegira![21]

Thus, he turned the building into a symbol for a 'third space' in past and present. Additions were celebrated as symbols of an ancient and ongoing encounter between cultures, almost erasing the idea that both the crusades and modern colonialism were built on war and conflict.

The Crac on the other hand was completely overhauled as a French National Monument following the energetic lobbying by Paul Deschamps, director of the Museum for French Monuments in Paris. The graduate of the École des Chartes almost became an 'accidental' crusader. Following the death of his mentor Camille Enlart, director of the Museum for Comparative Sculpture in Paris (before it was renamed Museum of French Monuments under Deschamps) and pioneering scholar of crusader architecture (who also conducted 'a very good friendship owing to the similarities of our tastes' with George Jeffery),[22] Deschamps was made Enlart's successor at the Trocadéro and in Syria.[23] While he knew little about military architecture when he went on his first mission to the Levant,[24] he ended up a self-styled crusader.[25] A devout Catholic, he was inspired by a romantic vision of the period and rejected any criticism of the crusaders as late as the 1970s.[26] During the French League of Nations' Mandate of Syria, Deschamps laboured tirelessly for the French government to obtain the Crac des Chevaliers, arguing that this 'essentially French monument' and 'national heritage'[27] needed to be rescued from the indigenous people, who used it as a quarry to build houses and lived on the site with their horses, donkeys, camels, cows, goats, and chicken. A village of 530 souls had grown inside the castle after the Ottoman district administration moved its seat to a more convenient location on the road to Homs in the late 1800s.[28] 'The Alawite State, on whose territory the Krak is situated, not being interested in this most important and best conserved of the castles constructed by the French, the only way to save is, is to acquire it.'[29]

The French Foreign Office negotiated that the Alawite State would offer the Crac as a gift to the French State, subject to one million Franks as indemnities for the expulsion of the indigenous inhabitants (an offer that was doubled from the initial 500,000 francs after consultation with member of the Representative Council of the Government of Latakia).[30] The price (plus an additional 2.2 million Francs for restoration) was initially approved,[31] but then suddenly withdrawn because of the Depression. In their renewed campaign, Deschamps, the Fine Arts Administration and the Foreign Office underlined not only the importance of the site as French national heritage and the threat posed to it by the indigenous population but also pointed out that failure to acquire it would give way to the possibility of 'the Knights of Malta – that is to say Italy', claiming the site.[32] Its 'propagandistic value' in the end triumphed. The acquisition was accompanied by a vast publicity effort in France ranging from the 1931 Colonial Exhibition, the Colonial Museum, and the Museum of French Monuments to radio shows, popular books and reproduction on postcards and even chocolate advertisements in which Deschamps was a key broker to French and international audiences.[33] The ensuing restoration, which removed the settlers, destroyed their habitation and restored the site to its 'original' appearance, went against international standards which favoured the preservation of the status quo, rather than any removal or new additions. However, there are parallels elsewhere in Mandatory Syria, Lebanon, and Palestine, most notably in Palmyra, where an even more substantial Ottoman village was relocated from inside the temple of Bel.[34]

Superficially the different treatments of the cathedral mosque of Famagusta and the Crac points to different attitudes towards the crusader past as a 'shared history' versus a 'national history' in British versus French (and Italian) imperial discourse. But a closer look at the main characters shows that in their wider writings Deschamps and Jeffery (who knew and appreciated each other and were linked through their personal connection with Enlart) expressed relatively similar ideas. In some of their writings both emphasised the essential Englishness and Frenchness of crusader sites, respectively. Elsewhere both used the crusades to highlight long lasting interactions between the West and the East and praised the resulting enmeshing of language, culture, and architecture.[35]

A deeper look also reveals that their room for manoeuvre, and the discourses they adopted, were shaped by other factors too. Their brokerage was framed by a greater will of the treasury in Paris than in London to fund the preservation of historic sites. Moreover, Deschamps came from the heart of the Parisian scholarly establishment and skilfully manipulated international competition and the fear of Fascist Italy's rise in the Mediterranean. Jeffery also tried to use foreign opinion. He likely authored a string of articles in the Italian press at the beginning of the century complaining about the English treatment of monuments in Cyprus, which he then forwarded to his contacts in London, who used them to argue that a change in English policies was needed to prevent loss of reputation abroad.[36] But these letters had little impact at the time. It was only after the French Foreign Ministry (despite Deschamps' trying to dissuade them) intervened upon the Foreign Office offering to buy the neglected monuments of 'French origin' in Cyprus in the mid-1930s that a better institutional framework and funding were provided in a context of rising anti-colonial nationalism.

Moreover, the elderly Jeffery was increasingly isolated in Cyprus as a younger generation of London educated scholars were trying to get him fired, retired (again with the help of the French) or at least limit his sphere influence to the monuments under the auspices of the Evcaf.[37] Described in the diaries of a contemporary Swedish traveller as looking 'like Darwin. But more congenial' with a love of cheap wine and home-made cigars,[38] his protracted speech and nervous manner caused people to dislike him. Increasingly lonely after the death of his wife, he lived alone with two servants in a dilapidated house in Nicosia threatened with destruction by the Mayor.[39] He had few Greek Cypriot friends and felt threatened by the suggestion of employing a Cypriot assistant. At a time when Governor Ronald Storrs pushed the employ of Greek Cypriots to Civil Service posts to strengthen relations with the community, Jeffery believed that if he were to be succeeded by a Greek Cypriot the work he had done for three decades for the medieval monuments of the island would be lost. He felt that the salary of the proposed candidate, Theophilus Moghabghab (1886–1965), a Surveying Engineer who was the son of the district medical officer of Famagusta and a Lebanese Christian who had graduated from the American University of Beirut, should be better spent on the monuments themselves as Moghabghab was 'not in any sense English beyond knowing the language he has never been in England and has no education as an archaeologist or what is of much greater importance as an architect'.[40] For Jeffery, any curator should be appointed by the Colonial Office, rather than by the Governor in Cyprus who could make small appointments without reference to London.[41] In the end however, it was Jeffery's post that was abolished in January 1935. He was appointed honorary advisor to the Department of Antiquities, under the new director J.R. Hilton. Moghabghab was transferred from the Government Land Office to the Department of Antiquities as an Antiquities Officer and Curator of Famagusta Museum. Like many of those involved in the restoration of crusader architecture, Moghabghab was later made an officer of the Venerable Order of Saint John.[42] The photographs with which he documented the restoration of medieval monuments,[43] give insights not only into architectural restoration but also into the lives of craftsmen, workers, and users.

Jeffery, meanwhile, found it easier to collaborate with the Muslim authorities overseeing historic mosques, especially the delegate of the Evcaf, Munir Bey (later Sir Mehmed Munir), than with the Greek Cypriots or the, in his eyes, philistine representatives of the British

Government in Cyprus. Hence the emphasis on the good level of collaboration between Muslims and Christians in the initial quote likely also served to refute criticism of his work and maintain his own position. While he judged 'Greeks' as viewing 'medieval churches and Castles with aversion as relics of foreign despotism – to be obliterated', he described 'Modern Turks' as the 'only Levantines who regard historic monuments of their own or any other country with any interest'.[44]

The majority of the medieval monuments of Cyprus, from the Hospitallers' Kolossi Castle, to the buildings erected under the Lusignan dynasty, were not government property but in private hands, those of the Orthodox Church or the Evcaf. Since the signing of the convention between the Ottoman Empire and Great Britain in 1878 which provided British support against war with Russia in exchange for the occupation and administration of Cyprus by Britain, the Evcaf appointed a Muslim inhabitant to supervise together with a delegate of the British authorities the administration of any property, endowments, and land that belonged to mosques, cemeteries, Muslim schools, and other religious establishments.[45] After the transformation of Cyprus into a Crown colony, the Evcaf went into the hands of the British in 1928. However it remained the most significant Turkish Cypriot organisation, and the delegate of the Evcaf, Munir Bey, is said to have been the most influential personality among the Turkish Cypriot community. The British administration compared him at times to an 'Old Ottoman pasha' with 'absolute power',[46] and at times to 'the indispensable and permanent Ataturk of Cyprus'[47] Resentment against him as a representative of an increasingly Anglicised Muslim elite through which the British government ruled rose, especially among Cypriot Kemalists,[48] and he lost his place on the legislative council in 1930.

Jeffery had been working closely with the Evcaf since his appointment to Cyprus. In 1906, Cecil Firth of the University of Oxford, whom the Society for the Protection of Ancient Buildings in London consulted on the matter of the medieval monuments of Cyprus, described the delegate of the Evcaf as 'a charming young man not unlike [the conservative politician and art connoisseur] Lord Balcarres to look at, only rather greyer. Speaks perfect English and drives the smartest pair in the island'. He also suggested the delegate had a 'considerable personal dislike of Mr. Jeffery which he would never let Jeffery see' and hence that Jeffery had little influence with the Evcaf.[49]

However, Jeffery's diary testified to a close collaboration in later times, with frequent entries about his work with Munir from 1926 onwards. Jeffery also introduced Munir to the Society for the Protection of Ancient Buildings in London, who subsequently made him an honorary member. In 1932, the Curator of Ancient Monuments also recommended Munir as 'a great friend and patron of mine' to the aforementioned Earl of Crawford and Balcarres[50] and to Hugh Sadler Kingsford of the Society of Antiquaries:

> like many modern Turks he takes a keen interest in the historic monuments and in archaeology generally. He has done an immense deal for Cyprus in this way. He is ex-officio a Guardian of all the Latin Cathedrals and churches and other buildings confiscated by the Turks in 1570, the Turkish member of the Cyprus Museum. I should like you as well as Sir Charles Peers to see him as he may give you a clearer account of what we are doing in Cyprus than that you may have obtained lately from a different source.[51]

Following the meeting with Kingsford at Burlington House, Munir, wrote to his 'dear Mr. Jeffery' with 'best love and kind regards' about the Buckingham Palace Garden Party he attended and where he was presented to the Duke and Duchess of York ('charming people'). He also made certain to report that he told Kingston with gratitude about all the things Jeffery had done for his department, explaining how carefully the 'Nicosia and Famagusta Cathedrals, Buyuk Medresse, and St. Catherine's etc.' had been handled, especially the minaret at Famagusta. While describing his own predecessor to Kingsford 'as a difficult man and nothing could be done', Munir indicated Jeffery 'had done wonders for us during the last 5 or 6 years'. In the context of talks about Jeffery's retirement, Munir rebuked that his friend was getting old instead suggesting 'that you were as energetic as a boy of 20 and that I could not compete with you […] I gave him to understand that you could go on for another 25 years'.[52]

In her fine-grained study of how the new British regime dealt with the legacy of traditional conservation practices of the waqf in Cyprus through an analysis of the archives of the Evcaf, Reyhan Sabri has shown the extent to which orientalist attitudes towards non-Western people and institutions were both patronising and ignorant. Consequently, she argues that there were few lessons drawn from the long history of effective conservation evident in the waqf properties, and ultimately a Western-authorised heritage discourse was established.[53] Conservation legislation was enacted to fight Greek nationalism, while the British administration used the Evcaf to strengthen the position of the Turkish-Muslim community. In Jeffery's own writing we can see, however, a shift from condemning traditional ways of dealing with Muslim architecture to an appreciation of the work of local craftsmen. This is most apparent when it comes to the building of the minarets on crusader churches. He described these unsympathetically as damaging to the buildings in a letter to the SPAB in 1904 but thirty years later responded positively to a petition to the Governor from Muslims of Famagusta about the addition of a minaret to the ex-cathedral of Famagusta.[54] He even argued that the west front lending itself to 'the exigencies of a Moslem mosque, whilst retaining all the characteristics of a great French church is certainly most wonderful'.[55] Whether such statements were motivated by a desire to appease the Turkish Cypriot community at a moment of nationalist tension, or to refute criticism from London of this own work with the Evcaf, or as a genuine celebration of the monuments of the crusades as hybrid monuments in past and present, the interactions demonstrate the complex human relations that shaped these discourses of hybridity. Meanwhile in Paris, Paul Deschamps edited most of the non-French contributions out of the record, despite the fact that the nationalisation of the crusades in France was also shaped by cross-cultural encounters. The recent scholarly and public interests in the French restoration in Syria – spurred by the possibility to use the interwar archives in the reconstruction of destroyed monuments in the Syrian civil war – reproduces the colonial logic of labelling indigenous inhabitants largely as destroyers and follows mainly Deschamps' own acknowledgement of collaborators when discussing the history of the Crac.[56] He primarily mentioned Camille Enlart, René Dussaud of the Louvre, Charles Virolleaud of the Antiquities Service in Syria, the architects François Anus and Pierre Coupel,[57] his 'comrade' Captain Lamblin, Captain Petit who provided arial photography, and the French army of the Levant (which included 60 Alawite soldiers) who helped to clear the castle.[58]

However, the archival record tells a more complex story. Despite the derogative language towards the villagers and the failure to publicly acknowledge intermediaries mentioned in his diaries (such as the translators used to access Arabic historic sources or communicate on site),[59] and his fiercely nationalist tone towards other Europeans, Deschamps was among a small group of friends who came to the defence of Jeffery against the concerted international effort to oust him. Deschamps also intervened for decades on behalf of the Guardian of the Crac, Assad Abbas. He wrote repeatedly to the Antiquities Service to remind them to pay Assad Abbas' (and his brother Abdou's) salary (Assad and Abdou's fee together was at 600 francs to the architects 5,000), supported increases due to the devaluation of the Franc and the rising cost of living, and pushed the Syrian government after independence to recognise the years in French employ for Assad Abbas' pension.[60] Perhaps Deschamps sympathised with the fact that Assad Abbas, like Deschamps, was the father of an increasing number of children whom he found it hard to provide for.[61] The sources tell us little about their relationship, but Deschamps' photographic collection contains many labelled photographs of Assad Abbas.

Assad Abbas lived in a 'locale' added during the restoration in the hard-to-get-to castle at the top of a mountain range with his brother Abdou, also made a guardian in the late 1930s. In the end, Assad Abbas was the most constant 'go-between' for the site, the workers and the authorities, across war and regime changes. Already guiding the visitors free of charge before the castle became the property of France,[62] he continued to guide thousands of tourists during the 1930s and many soldiers on leave during the Second World War.[63] Assad Abbas regularly wrote in Arabic via the Drogmanat to the Antiquities Service about repairs needed to the castle. He reported who visited and asked for promotional material, even offering to purchase postcards from his own funds, so that these could be sold to tourists.[64] He was first paid by the Government of Latakia, then by the French Republic, then by Vichy, and eventually by independent Syria. Changes in ownership generally entailed missed payments. A lack of funds was particularly acute during the Second World War but both Assad and his brother Abdou continued to work diligently without being paid. As the Director of Antiquities highlighted in January 1941, money had to be found. One could not dismiss them, as their work was paramount for the safety and upkeep of the historic monument.[65]

Conclusion: brokers, intermediaries, and go-betweens in the modern making of the crusades

Taken together the very brief and incomplete vignettes presented here confirm this book's central premise that the crusades despite their 'intrinsic internationalism', have long been conscripted for nationalist ends in the modern era. Yet this recruitment also happened through encounters and exchanges across cultural and national borders, adding further to the incongruity.

The complexity of these interactions can help to show that the tensions between nationalism and internationalism in the present – be it the incitement of nationalist violence through invocations of a shared heritage under attack from the extreme right or ISIS[66] or in the tendency of many national heritage bodies to focus on the multi-national nature of the crusades as a source for internationalism in the present – have a long history.⁶⁷ If one wants to understand and address these present tensions, it is helpful to take a closer look at the processes and actors that 'revived' the crusades in these manners and whose legacy lives on.⁶⁸

This chapter has attempted to locate different individuals in place and space to test how the concept of 'cultural brokers' might help to better understand the multitude of cross-cultural interactions that shaped the transformation of architecture left by the crusades into 'cultural heritage'. Let us conclude with questions that emerge from the case studies for a debate on broader conceptual reflections regarding the circulation of objects, people, and ideas in the modern memory of the crusades. I am conscious that I have only focussed in part on the classic 'go-between' identified by Kapil Raj and have merged the typologies developed by Alida Metcalf distinguishing between physical, transactional, and representational forms.⁶⁹ There is a need to look in more depth at individuals with a greater range in backgrounds, professions, and more limited power, but by applying the concept to those who shaped representational forms physically and through transactions (who are usually seen as the main heritage makers in the literature), and situate them in relation to their wider networks of less known brokers, intermediaries, and users one can glimpse both the range and the limits of agency.

Having used the terms 'cultural brokers', 'intermediaries', and 'go-betweens' loosely for individuals that move and mediate between cultures and through their actions change (them), I am wondering how useful it is to think of them as 'third parties' (Kapil Raj) or 'third elements' (Georg Simmel).⁷⁰ As has been pointed out in a related debate about comparative history versus intercultural transfers and *histoire croisée*, such labels assume the pre-existence of rather monolithic cultural or entities, which are then changed by a one-time interaction.⁷¹ This might work for some contexts – but it appears not useful for the one discussed here, where contacts were longstanding and ongoing. Moreover, by focussing in part on individuals with a strong standing in the colonial system, it becomes apparent that the intermediaries were not a separate group but moved in and out of different intermediary roles and cultures, with different levels of power at different times. There are certainly a number of individuals who performed more cross-cultural mediation than others, but given the highly entangled nature of heritage-making (both in conceptual and physical terms) in the nineteenth and twentieth centuries virtually all those involved in the process of producing and consuming the crusades and their sites were also in some ways involved in acts of 'cultural brokerage'. The result does not appear to be one 'space in between' but many different metaphorical and geographical spaces whose producers, users, and intermediaries deserve further investigation.

Notes

1 I am grateful for the support of the British Academy and the Paul Mellon Centre for British Art for their support for the research underpinning this article and to Mike Horswell for his insightful comments.
2 For a recent historiographic discussion see Jonathan Phillips and Mike Horswell, 'Introduction' in *Engaging the Crusades, Vol. 1*, pp. 1–6, as well as the ensuing volumes of the *Engaging the Crusades* series.
3 See for instance Elizabeth Siberry, 'Images of the Crusades in the Nineteenth and Twentieth Centuries' in Jonathan Riley-Smith (ed.), *The Oxford Illustrated History of the Crusades* (Oxford, 1995); Ronnie Ellenblum, *Crusader Castles and Modern Histories* (Cambridge, 2007), Astrid Swenson, 'Crusader Heritages and Imperial Preservation' *Past & Present* 226 (2015) sup. 10, pp. 27–56; Mike Horswell, Andrew Jotischky, Thomas Simpson, and Astrid Swenson, 'Vectors of Memory: Modern Material Memories of the Crusader States' in *The Material Culture of the Crusader States: A Handbook*, eds. Elizabeth Lapina, Adrian Boas, and Nicholas Morton (forthcoming).
4 Jane Caplan, *'Jetzt judenfrei': Writing Tourism in Nazi-Occupied Poland* (London, 2013), p. 5.
5 Kurt Villads Jensen, Kirsi Salonen, and Helle Vogt (eds.), *Cultural Encounters During the Crusades* (Odense, 2013).
6 Knobler, 'Holy Wars'; Siberry, *New Crusaders*; Horswell, *British Crusader Medievalism*; Elizabeth Siberry, *Tales of the Crusaders – Remembering the Crusades in Britain: Engaging the Crusades, Volume Six* (Abingdon, 2021).
7 Kapil Raj, 'Go-Betweens, Travelers, and Cultural Translators', in *A Companion to the History of Science,* ed. Bernard Lightman (Oxford: 2016), p. 41.
8 For an overview see Paul Betts and Corey Ross, 'Modern Historical Preservation – Towards a Global Perspective', *Past & Present* 226 (2015), pp. 7–26.
9 Reyhan Sabri, *The Imperial Politics of Architectural Conservation* (Basingstoke, 2019); Billie Melman, *Empires of Antiquities* (Oxford, 2020); Mirjam Brusius, *The Empire in Storage* (Oxford, forthcoming).
10 See Laura Jane Smith, *Uses of Heritage* (Abingdon, 2006).
11 Luigi Pernier to Georg Karo, Rome 18 Aug 1913 (copy): Rome, Archivio Centrale dello Stato, MPI, Direzione generale delle antichità e belle arti, Gen. AA. BB, AA, Dir, I, 1908–1924, Busta 618.
12. 'Editorial, Prof. Luigi Pernier', *Nature* 140 (18 September 1937), pp. 495–96.
13 See Astrid Lindenlauf, 'Karo, Georg Heinrich', in Peter Kuhlmann, Helmuth Schneider (eds.), *Geschichte der Altertumswissenschaften: Biographisches Lexikon* (*Der Neue Pauly*, suppl. 6) (Stuttgart/Weimar, 2012), cols. 641 f.
14 For context see Simona Troilo, '"A Gust of Cleansing Wind": Italian Archaeology on Rhodes and in Libya in the Early Years of Occupation (1911–1914)', *Journal of Modern Italian Studies* 17 (2012), pp. 45–69.
15 Ibid., p. 57.

16 The discussion here draws on the exchange between Pernier and Karo between 18 and 31 August 1913, Rome, Archivio Centrale dello Stato, MPI, Direzione generale delle antichità e belle arti, Gen. AA. BB, AA, Dir, I, 1908–1924, Busta 618. On the Danish accusations see also Ricci to Ministero della Guerra (Minister of War), 4 January 1913. In ACS, MPI, AABBAA, Div. I, 1908–1924, b. 618.
17 Georgios Karatzas, 'On the Physical and Discursive Articulation of the Heritage Space of the City of Rhodes (1912 – 1967)', *Journal of Mediterranean Studies* 28 (2019), pp. 33–53.
18 Pierre Pinon, 'Albert Gabriel et la restauration de l'Auberge de France à Rhodes', *Bulletin Monumental* 175 (2017), pp. 245–51.
19 The National Archives, Kew, FO 608/102/12.
20 Despina Pilides, *George Jeffery: His Diaries and the Ancient Monuments of Cyprus*, 2 vols. (Lefkosia, 2009), p. 83.
21 Report by George Jeffery on 'Famagusta, Cyprus, The Great Mosque', 1934, Nicosia, Cyprus State Archives (CSA), SAI/992/34.
22 George Jeffery, 'Autobiographical Notes' (1920), in Pilides (ed.), *Jeffery*, I, p. 83; George Jeffery to Secretary of the SPAB, 24 June 1901, in ibid., II, pp. 596–97. On government assistance to French scholars, AN, F17/2960, Mission de Camille Enlart en Chypre; Heiniker-Heaton (C.S.) to Consul of France, 25 Jan. 1933, CSA, SAI 431/33.
23 Jean Richard, 'Notice sur la vie et les travaux de Paul Deschamps, Membre de l'Académie', *Comptes-rendus des séances de l'Académie des inscriptions et belles-lettres* 135 (1991), pp. 336–46.
24 Quoted in ibid., p. 342.
25 According to Gustave Dupont-Ferrier quoted in ibid., p. 345. See also *Remise a M. Paul Deschamps de son Epée d'Academicien, le 26 Octobre 1943 au Musée des Monuments Français*, Paris, Archives des Musée nationaux (AMN), O30 471 Paul Deschamps (now Archives Nationales).
26 Richard, 'Notice sur la vie', p. 345.
27 The expression '*patrimoine national*' is recurrent in Deschamps's letters to various government agencies involved in the negotiations and was taken up by the Administration des Beaux-Arts, Paris, Mediathèque de l'architecture et du Patrimoine (MAP), 81/98/3, 'Syrie, Acquisition du Krak'.
28 Stefan H. Winter, 'Le Crac des Chevaliers et le village de Hisn al-Akrad à l'époque ottoman', in Jean-Marc Hofman and Emmanuel Pénicaut (eds.), *Le Crac des Chevaliers* (Paris, 2018), pp. 33–42.
29 Sous-Secrétariat des eaux-arts to Minister of Foreign Affairs, 1 April 1931, in Archives des Affaires étrangères, La Courneuve (AAE Courneuve), Correspondance Politique et Commerciale E, Levant, Syrie, Liban, 1918–1940, 50 CPCOM/601, Microfilm 2393, fol 36–37.
30 Delegate of the High Commissioner to Minister for Foreign Affairs, 30 Oct. 1931, AAE Courneuve, 50 CPCOM/601, Microfilm 2393, fol 51.
31 'Project de loi ayant pour objet l'acquisition par l'Etat du Crac des Chevaliers appartenant a l'Etat des Alaouites (Syrie)', MAP, 81/98/3, 'Syrie, Acquisition du Krak'.

32 Presidence du Conseil, Affaires Etrangères to Sous-Secretaire D'Etat des Beaux-Arts, 8 Dec 1932, MAP, 81/98/3, 'Syrie Aquisition du Krak'. For the details of the acquisition, Centre des Archives Diplomatiques Nantes (CADN), 188PO/C/30-33 Damas (ambassade), Séries C Biens français en Syrie Krak des Chevaliers, AAE Courneuve 50CPCOM/601.
33 On international reception: 'The Crusaders Greatest Castle Ceded to France for Preservation', *Illustrated London News*, 20 Oct 1934, p. iv.
34 Mirjam Brusius, 'Objects and History Adrift: Contextualizing the debate about Middle Eastern "Heritage"', in: *Das verirrte Kunstwerk*, U. Fleckner and E. Tolstichin (eds.) (Berlin, 2019), pp. 55–71.
35 On Deschamps's praises of what we would now call hybridity see Exposition coloniale internationale de Paris 1931, Commissariat General, *Les Colonies et la vie française pendant huit siècles* (Paris, 1933).
36 Pilides, *Jeffery*, I, pp. 20–21.
37 See despatches 1931–34, CADN, 345 PO1 Larnaca, Consulat et Agence Consulaire.
38 Quoted in Pilides, *Jeffery*, I. p. 74.
39 Ibid., I. p. 14.
40 George Jeffery, Draft of unfinished letter to the Secretary of the SPAB, Peers, reprinted in Pilides, *Jeffery*, II, p. 402.
41 Ibid., I, p. 16.
42 *The London Gazette,* 10 January 1958.
43 James Kusch, *Knowledge, Differences and Identity in the Time of Globalization* (Newcastle, 2011), pp. 121–22.
44 G. Jeffery to Lord Crawford, Nicosia 30 June 1932, Jeffery papers, Foolscap Manuscript Book 8, in Pilides, *Jeffery*, II, p. 615.
45 Bernhard Hofstötter, 'Cyprus under British Rule: An International Law Analysis of Certain Land Surveys and Land Assignment Between 1878 and 1955', *Chinese Journal of International Law* 7 (2008), pp. 159–96.
46 Jeanette Choisi, 'The Turkish Cypriot Elite – Its Social Function and Legitimation', *The Cyprus Review* 5 (1993), p. 14.
47 Ronald Storrs, *Orientations* (London, 1943), pp. 492–93.
48 Charles Fraser Beckingham, 'Islam and Turkish Nationalism Cyprus', *Die Welt des Islam* new series 5 (1957), pp. 65–83.
49 Pilides, *Jeffery*, I, p. 30 and II, pp. 606–07.
50 Jeffery to Lord Crawford, Nicosia 30 June 1932, in Pilides, *Jeffery*, II, p. 615.
51 Jeffery to Kingsford, in ibid., II, p. 616.
52 Munir to Jeffery, London, 2 Aug 1932, in ibid., II, p. 616.
53 Sabri, *Imperial Politics*, p. 11.
54 Jeffery to the delegates of Evcaf, Nicosia 17 Sep 1931, in Pilides, *Jeffery*, II, p. 571.
55 Jeffery 'The Great Mosque', CSA, SAI/992/34.
56 Hofman and Pénicaut, *Crac des Chevaliers*.
57 AMN, Paris, Serie O, 030471 Paul Deschamps.
58 Clement Moussé, 'Paul Deschamps e la prospection aérienne aux Pays du Levant', *Bibliothèque de l'Institut national d'histoire de l'art,* 28 June 2016, <https://web.archive.org/web/20220901092434/https://blog.bibliotheque.inha.fr/fr/posts/paul-deschamps-prospection-aerienne-pays-du-levant.html>, [accessed 1 September 2022].

59 INHA, Paris, Fonds Deschamps.
60 Paul Deschamps to George Daulalty, Beyrout 6 December 1937, in CADN, 188PO/C/30.
61 AMN, Paris, Serio O, 030471 Paul Deschamps.
62 Schoeffler, Gouverneur de Lattaquie, to comte de Martel, Ambassadeur haut commisaire de la République francaise en Syrie et au Liban, Service des Antiquités, Lattaquie, 23 Nov. 1933.
63 CADN, 188PO/C/30-33; INHR, Fonds Paul Deschamps; MAP, Fond Paul Deschamps (photographic collection).
64 Assad Abbas to Haut Commissariat de la République française en Syrie et au Liban, Drogmanat, Kalaat El Hosn, 12 Jan. 1928, CADN, 188PO/C/30.
65 CADN, 188PO/C/30.
66 Charlotte Gauthier and Jonathan Phillips (eds.), *The Crusades and the Far-Right: Engaging the Crusades, Volume Nine* (Abingdon: Routledge, forthcoming).
67 Raj, 'Go-Betweens', p. 41.
68 Kristin Skottki, 'The Dead, the Revived and the Recreated Pasts: "Structural Amnesia" in Representations of Crusade History', in *Engaging the Crusades, Vol. 1*, pp. 107–32.
69 Raj, 'Go-Betweens', p. 41.
70 Ibid.
71 Michael Werner and Bénédicte Zimmermann, 'Penser l'histoire croisée: entre empirie et réflexivité', *Annales* 58 (2003), pp. 7–36.

Bibliography

Primary – Manuscript

Archives des Affaires étrangères, La Courneuve (AAE Courneuve). Correspondance Politique et Commerciale E, Levant, Syrie, Liban, 1918–1940. 50 CPCOM/601, Microfilm 2393.
Archives des Musée nationaux Paris (AMN). O30 471. Paul Deschamps.
Archives Nationales Pierrefite (AN). F17/2960. Mission de Camille Enlart en Chypre.
Centre des Archives diplomatiques de Nantes (CADN). 188PO/C/30-33.
Cyprus State Archives Nicosia (CSA). SAI 431/33.
Institut National d'Histoire de l'Art, Paris (INHA). Fonds Deschamps.
Mediathèque de l'architecture et du Patrimoine, Paris (MAP). 81/98/3 'Syrie, Acquisition du Krak'.
Rome, Archivio Centrale dello Stato, MPI, Direzione generale delle antichità e belle arti. Gen. AA. BB, AA, Dir, I, 1908–1924, Busta 618.
The National Archives, Kew (TNA). FO 608/102/12.

Primary – Printed

'Editorial, Prof. Luigi Pernier'. *Nature* 140 (18 September 1937), pp. 495–96.

Exposition coloniale internationale de Paris 1931. Commissariat General, *Les Colonies et la vie française pendant huit siècles*. Paris, 1933.
Storrs, Ronald. *Orientations*. London: Nicholson and Watson, 1943.
'The Crusaders' Greatest Castle Ceded to France for Preservation'. *Illustrated London News*. 20 Oct 1934, p. iv.

Secondary

Beckingham, Charles Fraser. 'Islam and Turkish Nationalism Cyprus'. *Die Welt des Islam new series* 5 (1957), pp. 65–83.
Betts, Paul and Corey Ross. 'Modern Historical Preservation – Towards a Global Perspective'. *Past & Present* 226 (2015), pp. 7–26.
Brusius, Mirjam. 'Objects and History Adrift: Contextualizing the debate about Middle Eastern "Heritage"'. In *Das verirrte Kunstwerk. Bedeutung, Funktion und Manipulation von "Bilderfahrzeugen" in der Diaspora*. Eds. U. Fleckner and E. Tolstichin. Berlin: München De Gruyter, 2019, pp. 55–71.
———. *The Empire in Storage: Objects Without Status between Middle Eastern Excavation Sites and Europe's Museums*. Oxford: OUP, forthcoming.
Caplan, Jane. *'Jetzt judenfrei': Writing Tourism in Nazi-Occupied Poland*. London: German Historical Institute, 2013.
Choisi, Jeanette. 'The Turkish Cypriot Elite – Its Social Function and Legitimation'. *The Cyprus Review* 5 (1993), pp. 7–26.
Ellenblum, Ronnie. *Crusader Castles and Modern Histories*. Cambridge: Cambridge University Press, 2007.
Gauthier, Charlotte, and Jonathan Phillips, eds. *The Crusades and the Far-Right: Engaging the Crusades, Volume Nine*. Abingdon: Routledge, forthcoming.
Hinz, Felix, and Johannes Meyer-Hamme, eds. *Controversial Histories – Current Views on the Crusades: Engaging the Crusades, Volume Three*. Abingdon: Routledge, 2020.
Hofman, Jean-Marc, and Emmanuel Pénicaut, eds. *Le Crac des Chevaliers. Chroniques d'un rêve en pierre*. Paris: Hermann 2018, pp. 33–42.
Hofstötter, Bernhard. 'Cyprus under British Rule: An International Law Analysis of Certain Land Surveys and Land Assignment Between 1878 and 1955'. *Chinese Journal of International Law* 7 (2008), pp. 159–96.
Horswell, Mike. *The Rise and Fall of British Crusader Medievalism, c. 1825–1945*. Abingdon: Routledge, 2018.
Horswell, Mike, Andrew Jotischky, Thomas Simpson, and Astrid Swenson. 'Vectors of Memory: Modern Material Memories of the Crusader States'. In *The Material Culture of the Crusader States: A Handbook*. Eds. Adrian Boas, Elizabeth Lapina, and Nicholas Morton. Abingdon: Routledge, forthcoming.
Jensen, Kurt Villads, Kirsi Salonen and Helle Vogt, eds. *Cultural Encounters During the Crusades*. Odense: University Press of Southern Denmark, 2013.
Karatzas, Georgios. 'On the Physical and Discursive Articulation of the Heritage Space of the City of Rhodes (1912 – 1967)'. *Journal of Mediterranean Studies* 28 (2019), pp. 33–53.

Knobler, Adam. 'Holy Wars, Empires, and the Portability of the Past: The Modern Uses of Medieval Crusades'. *Comparative Studies in Society and History* 48 (2006), pp. 293–325.

Kusch, James. *Knowledge, Differences and Identity in the Time of Globalization: Institutional Discourse and Practices.* Newcastle: Cambridge Scholars Publishing, 2011.

Lindenlauf, Astrid. 'Karo, Georg Heinrich'. In *Geschichte der Altertumswissenschaften: Biographisches Lexikon* (*Der Neue Pauly*, suppl. 6). Eds. Peter Kuhlmann, and Helmuth Schneider. Stuttgart/Weimar: Metzler, 2012, cols. 641 f.

Melman, Billie. *Empires of Antiquities: Modernity and the Rediscovery of the Ancient Near East, 1914–1950.* Oxford: OUP, 2020.

Moussé, Clement. 'Paul Deschamps e la prospection aérienne aux Pays du Levant'. *Bibliothèque de l'Institut national d'histoire de l'art.* 28 June 2016. https://web.archive.org/web/20220901092434/https://blog.bibliotheque.inha.fr/fr/posts/paul-deschamps-prospection-aerienne-pays-du-levant.html. Accessed 1 September 2022.

Pilides, Despina. *George Jeffery: His Diaries and the Ancient Monuments of Cyprus.* 2 vols. Lefkosia: Department of Antiquities, Ministry of Communications and Works, Republic of Cyprus, 2009.

Phillips, Jonathan, and Mike Horswell. 'Introduction'. In *Perceptions of the Crusades from the Nineteenth to the Twenty-First Century: Engaging the Crusades, Volume One.* Eds. Mike Horswell and Jonathan Phillips. Abingdon: Routledge, 2018, pp. 1–6.

Pinon, Pierre. 'Albert Gabriel et la restauration de l'Auberge de France à Rhodes'. *Bulletin Monumental* 175 (2017), pp. 245–51.

Raj, Kapil. 'Go-Betweens, Travelers, and Cultural Translators'. In *A Companion to the History of Science.* Ed. Bernard Lightman. Oxford: Wiley Blackwell, 2016, pp. 35–57.

Richard, Jean. 'Notice sur la vie et les travaux de Paul Deschamps, Membre de l'Académie'. *Comptes-rendus des séances de l'Académie des inscriptions et belles-lettres* 135 (1991), pp. 336–46.

Sabri, Reyhan. *The Imperial Politics of Architectural Conservation: The Case of Waqf in Cyprus.* Basingstoke: Palgrave Macmillan, 2019.

Siberry, Elizabeth. 'Images of the Crusades in the Nineteenth and Twentieth Centuries'. In *The Oxford Illustrated History of the Crusades.* Ed. Jonathan Riley-Smith. Oxford: OUP, 1995, pp. 365–85.

———. *The New Crusaders: Images of the Crusades in the 19th and Early 20th Centuries.* Aldershot: Ashgate, 2000.

———. *Tales of the Crusaders – Remembering the Crusades in Britain: Engaging the Crusades, Volume Six.* Abingdon: Routledge, 2021.

Skottki, Kristin. 'The Dead, the Revived and the Recreated Pasts: "Structural Amnesia" in Representations of Crusade History'. In *Perceptions of the Crusades from the Nineteenth to the Twenty-First Century: Engaging the Crusades, Volume One.* Eds. Mike Horswell and Jonathan Phillips. Abingdon: Routledge, 2018, pp. 107–32.

Smith, Laura Jane. *Uses of Heritage*. Abingdon: Routledge, 2006.
Swenson, Astrid. 'Crusader Heritages and Imperial Preservation'. *Past and Present* 226 (2015), sup. 10, pp. 27–56.
Troilo, Simona. '"A Gust of Cleansing Wind": Italian Archaeology on Rhodes and in Libya in the Early Years of Occupation (1911–1914)'. *Journal of Modern Italian Studies* 17 (2012), pp. 45–69.
Werner, Michael, and Bénédicte Zimmermann. 'Penser l'histoire croisée: entre empirie et réflexivité'. *Annales* 58 (2003), pp. 7–36.
Winter, Stefan H. 'Le Crac des Chevaliers et le village de Hisn al-Akrad à l'époque ottoman'. In *Le Crac des Chevaliers. Chroniques d'un rêve en pierre*. Eds. Jean-Marc Hofman and Emmanuel Pénicaut. Paris: Hermann 2018, pp. 33–42.

5 Bushido, Chivalry, and the Crusades in Japan from the 1870s to the First World War

Oleg Benesch

Introduction

As in much of the world, the crusades and the medieval European knight were powerful symbols in Japan at the turn of the twentieth century.[1] This may at first glance seem surprising given Japan's lack of a direct historical connection to the crusades or medieval Europe. As I argue in this chapter, however, the crusades were a significant concept in the social, religious, and cultural dynamics of the Meiji (1868–1912) and Taisho (1912–26) periods, and influenced Japan's evolving relationship with the rest of the world. I further contend that consideration of the crusades in Japan should be seen as part of a response to, and participation in, a larger global medievalist moment that reached virtually all societies in some form in the decades before the First World War. Throughout, I use the concept of 'medievalism' to refer to the use of medieval symbols and ideas in contexts removed in time and/ or space from the Middle Ages and 'medievalising' to emphasise the active processes by which a 'medieval' past is 'made' rather than 'found'. Alongside the expansion of European empires and their projects of imperial knowledge-making, Western medievalists and other figures sought to discover or assign a 'medieval' past to non-European societies. Japanese intellectuals and leaders first internalised this medievalising project and thereby contributed to the internationalisation of the crusades as part of their participation in a supposed shared medievalist heritage, before nationalising *against* the crusades and the European Middle Ages to create a new Japanese medieval identity. This study focuses on the period from the broad dissemination of the concept of the crusades in Japan in the 1870s to the relative decline of the universal European medievalist model around the time of the First World War.

Mike Horswell has argued for the rise and fall of 'crusader medievalism' in Britain during the nineteenth and early twentieth centuries

DOI: 10.4324/9781003241935-6

Bushido, Chivalry, and the Crusades in Japan 99

as an important part of the broader revival of medievalist symbols and themes in almost all areas of art, culture, and society.² In Japan, arguably Britain's closest ally from the time of the Anglo-Japanese Alliance in 1902 through the end of the First World War in 1918, crusade narratives were influenced by a range of interrelated factors. Images of the crusades were introduced, interrogated, and sustained in various spheres of Japanese society, including (as will be shown) education, diplomacy, and religion. At the same time, discussions of the crusades were firmly entangled with emerging debates around the concept of the 'medieval' more generally, and the popularisation of the concept of bushido (*bushidō*; the 'way of the warrior' or 'way of the samurai') from the 1890s onward. These debates were in turn closely tied to the search for a new national identity in Japan that drew on both foreign models and native traditions – real and invented.

In the nineteenth century, especially in popular discourse, it was not always possible to clearly separate the concepts of knights, chivalry, and the crusades.³ This continued to be the case as the crusades became more closely aligned with modern nationalism from the 1830s onward, when they were claimed by existing and emerging European nations.⁴ The crusades were also increasingly seen as an essential formative influence on European knighthood and chivalry, a notion that was reinforced by popular literature that was often set in the Holy Land or incorporated crusading themes such as knights and kings returned from crusade. This correlation was taken up in Japan, where the crusades were portrayed as the crucible of, and inseparable from, European knighthood and chivalry. Japanese responses to this amalgam can be seen to replicate the shape of this European medievalism, including the indistinct borders of chivalry and crusading: Japanese discussions of European (especially British) strength alighted upon a perceived continuity of medieval spirit in the form of chivalry, of which the crusader knight was an exemplar. In turn, through the invocation of bushido and the samurai, Japanese thinkers attempted to resurrect elements of an imagined, newly designated 'medieval' past in order to address perceived present deficiencies. The crusades, then, figured both directly and obliquely in Japanese thinking between the last decades of the nineteenth-century and the First World War.

This chapter has three parts. It begins by discussing Japan's engagement with what I call the 'global medievalist moment' that began in the late nineteenth century, and considers how European models were entangled with the rediscovery and rehabilitation of Japan's historic samurai warriors. The second section looks at the influence of crusader and chivalric heritage on diplomacy, especially between Japan and Britain. The third part considers the unique role played by Japanese Christians in the dissemination of bushido discourse in Japan, as well as the promotion of Japanese medievalism abroad.

Samurai, bushido, and medievalism

> To have lived through the transition stage of modern Japan makes a man feel preternaturally old; for here he is in modern times, with the air full of talk about Darwinism, and phonographs, and parliamentary institutions, and yet he can himself distinctly remember the Middle Ages [...] The Japanese boast that they have done in twenty years what it took Europe half as many centuries to accomplish.[5]
>
> (Basil Hall Chamberlain, 1891)

This study uses the concept of 'medievalism' to designate the use, revival, and reinterpretation of ideas and symbols associated with a perceived Middle Ages; indeed, with the creation of a medieval period itself. Definitions of 'medievalism' often focus on temporality, specifically the use of the medieval after the end of the (European) Middle Ages. If, however, one considers medievalism on a global scale, we see that people in Western nations were 'medievalising' their contemporaries, especially in the colonised world. In Japan, Chamberlain and his contemporaries – foreign and Japanese – were engaged in a 'medievalising' process.

Modern medievalist movements in Europe have been widely studied over the past century, especially in Britain, France, and Germany.[6] More recently, attention has turned to uses of medievalism in the former European settler colonies in the Americas, Australia, and elsewhere.[7] In a separate development, scholars in the early twenty-first century have begun to examine the application of the medieval paradigm to non-Western societies, examining the possibilities and limitations of a 'global Middle Ages'.[8] In contrast, the study of *medievalism* has not been systematically extended beyond Europe and some of its former imperial possessions. As the case of Japan illustrates, however, a 'global medievalist moment' from the mid-nineteenth to mid-twentieth centuries influenced many societies in a complex entanglement of ideas that often decentred Europe.

In Europe, interest in an idealised medieval past grew slowly before accelerating rapidly with the proliferation of nationalist sentiment in the nineteenth century, with art, literature, and architecture celebrating medieval themes. Significantly, the medieval age also served as the inspiration for European nations' martial traditions, and was important not only in intra-European conflicts, but was instrumental in the imperial expansion of the European colonial powers. Soldiers and colonial administrators were often inspired by an idealised martial crusader past during their encounters with the societies they subjugated, and the colonisers frequently classified people in Asia, Africa, and elsewhere as being in a 'medieval' stage of development between 'primitive' and 'civilised'.[9]

This approach reflected a clear tension between negative understandings of the 'feudal' age as Europe's backward past – and many non-Western societies' present – and the positive invocation of medieval symbols and concepts as the basis for European nations' dominance, historical legitimacy, and martial prowess. This tension was at the heart of the global medievalist moment in the decades before the First World War, as Europe's exaltation of its medieval past was juxtaposed with its contemporary dominance built on the most modern military technologies. At the same time, many non-Western thinkers were attracted to the popular Social Darwinist theories in spite of their pejorative portrayal of their own societies, as they were predicated on the possibility of social evolution towards the 'civilisational' levels attained by the West.[10]

Outside Europe, the medievalist paradigm became increasingly influential, especially in the former European settler societies that attempted to build on an idealised medieval Europe to define their own identities. Medievalism also spread readily to areas that had been in direct contact with Europe during the medieval period, especially the regions around the Mediterranean that had been directly affected by the crusades. The increased popularity of Saladin (Salah ad-Din) in the Arab world in the late nineteenth century is one example of this.[11] Similarly, the Ottoman Empire became heavily invested in the medievalist project especially during the World's Fair in Vienna in 1873, where the Ottoman Pavilion was designed in a medievalist style based on Orientalist European portrayals of the past.[12] Further East, there were attempts to apply medievalist periodisation and models to many parts of Asia, including India and China. Academic and popular attempts to define a 'medieval' period in India, as elsewhere, were influenced by political, national, and religious agendas, and the applicability of the term 'medieval' to periods of Indian history continues to be a topic of debate.[13] In China, there were similar attempts to impose a Eurocentric periodisation on Chinese history, also with limited success.[14]

Medievalism arguably became most firmly established in Japan, which is frequently used as a non-Western comparative case study by scholars of the Middle Ages. As in Europe, the boundaries of the medieval period in Japanese history vary considerably, although the current scholarly consensus uses the four centuries from the end of the Heian period (794–1185) to the unification of Japan by the Tokugawa shogunate (1603–1868). In this context, in both Japanese and Western scholarship, the medieval is closely entangled with the concept of 'feudalism' in popular understandings, even if its meaning and applicability to both Japan and Europe is debated.[15] In Japan, the term 'feudal' was often used retrospectively to describe society before major historical ruptures, especially the Meiji Restoration of 1868 and Japan's defeat in 1945.[16]

At the start of the Meiji period (1868–1912), an era known as the age of 'civilisation and enlightenment', the recent Tokugawa age was rejected as 'feudal' and backward; a classically pejorative characterisation of a 'medieval' period. Instead, Japan's leaders sought to make up more than one thousand years of European 'progress' in just a few decades. By the late 1870s, the rigid class structures of Tokugawa society had been abolished, the formerly elite samurai warriors lost their swords, stipends, and other privileges, and the vast majority of Japan's monumental historic castles were torn down as 'useless things'.[17] By the 1880s, increasing awareness of the idealised European past began to change attitudes, as competing visions of national identity sought to distinguish Japan from the traditional and new cultural hegemons, i.e., China and the West. This search for identity was informed and legitimised by similar European explorations of the proto-national past, especially the medieval period. Physical, spatial, visual, and textual encounters with European medievalism fed into re-evaluations of Japan's own history.

Already in the late Tokugawa period, Western history was a subject of considerable interest in Japan, and this increased greatly from the 1860s onward as more information became available and accessible. The famous educator and founder of the school that would later become Keio University, Fukuzawa Yukichi (1835–1901) was one of the first to discuss the crusades in his bestselling 1866 text *Conditions in the West* (*Seiyō jijō*).[18] With the establishment of a new education system in the early Meiji period, translations and summaries of Western textbooks on 'world history' proliferated, with the philosopher Nishi Amane (1829–97) coining the Japanese term for crusade, *jūjigun* ('cross army'), in his 1870 *Encyclopedia* (*Hyakugaku renkan*).[19]

By the 1870s, Japanese people would have had considerable access to knowledge about the crusades.[20] Translations of textbooks by authors such as Peter Parley (Samuel Goodrich, 1793–1860), William Cooke Taylor (1800–49), and William Swinton (1833–92) were the most influential sources for world – essentially Western – history until the turn of the twentieth century. These translated texts went into considerable detail, reflecting the significance of the crusades in the original; the 1878 translation of Taylor's *A Manual of Modern History*, for example, devoted 75 pages to the crusades.[21] Several elements of the crusade narratives in these Japanese texts are particularly relevant. One of these is that the crusades were generally depicted as the catalyst for chivalry to become fully formed and medieval knighthood to reach its apex.[22] As Taylor wrote in the *Manual*, 'Chivalry, though older than the crusades, derived its chief influence and strength from these wars. The use of surnames, coats of arms, and distinctive banners, became necessary in armies composed of men differing in language, habits, and feelings, collected at hazard from every Christian kingdom.'[23]

Another key aspect of crusade narratives from the perspective of Japanese readers was the notion that the crusades represented an extensive interaction between East and West, even if this was sometimes portrayed as a 'clash between races'.[24] More importantly, the crusades were seen as the moment when Europeans were exposed to 'Oriental' thought and culture, which had a lasting positive and even 'enlightening' effect.[25] As Parley's *Universal History* described it, 'the half barbarous inhabitants of Europe brought from the East many arts that tended to refine and civilise the people. In this, and other ways, the crusades produced some good results.'[26] This passage was accurately rendered in the Japanese translation published by the Japanese Ministry of Education in the 1870s.[27] Taylor's *Manual* presented the growth of commerce in the European Mediterranean and the development of the Hanseatic League as results of the crusades.[28] Furthermore, several texts causally linked the crusades to the subsequent 'spirit of adventurous navigation' that seemingly marked the rise to power of the European empires and led to their global dominance by the late nineteenth century.[29]

Inspired by the narratives of the crusades and chivalry that were a key part of the global medievalist moment, Japanese in the late 1880s began to rediscover their own 'medieval' past as a source for a modern national identity, and to place Japan into a chronological framework of progress that reflected European models.[30] The wholesale demolition of Japan's hundreds of obsolete castles ceased, while the gradual rehabilitation of the samurai heritage culminated in the creation of bushido as a counterpart to European chivalry. Contrary to popular perceptions, historians have shown that bushido is largely a modern construct with few direct connections to the premodern samurai, with the term '*bushidō*' only coming into widespread use in the late 1890s.[31]

Bushido was proposed not by conservative reactionaries, however, but by relatively progressive individuals with considerable international experience and a good command of one or more Western languages. The first modern writings on bushido by the influential journalist and later politician Ozaki Yukio (1858–1954) from 1888 onward posited the concept as a potential Japanese equivalent to the English ethic of 'gentlemanship', which was popularly traced back to medieval chivalry.[32] Books and articles on bushido began to be published increasingly after 1900, with the concept becoming a core part of the civilian and military education systems until the end of the Second World War in 1945.[33] Japanese thinkers from the late nineteenth century onward frequently engaged with more established discourses on European chivalry, going beyond mere translation of Western texts. As Nitobe Inazō (1862–1933) wrote in his 1900 bestseller *Bushido: The Soul of Japan*: 'Few historical comparisons can be more judiciously made than between the Chivalry of Europe and the Bushido of Japan'.[34] Indeed, since that time, many volumes have been published comparing knights and samurai in Japanese and Western languages (see Figs. 5.1 and 5.2).[35] Japan represents arguably the most comprehensive application of the medieval paradigm to a non-Western society.

Diplomacy

> If military interests had operated alone, without higher moral support, how far short of chivalry would the ideal of knighthood have fallen! In Europe, Christianity, interpreted with concessions convenient to chivalry, infused it nevertheless with spiritual data. 'Religion, war and glory were the three souls of a perfect Christian knight', says Lamartine.[36]
>
> (Nitobe Inazō, 1900)

For the leaders of the new Meiji government in 1868, the security of Japan was of paramount concern just as it had been for their Tokugawa predecessors. The collapse of the shogunal order was largely the result of domestic conflicts over how Japan should deal with the increasingly frequent foreign threats, especially after the arrival of the American

Bushido, Chivalry, and the Crusades in Japan   105

Figure 5.1 'Japanese warriors and religion' depicting the medieval warlord Katō Kiyomasa (1562–1611) in front of a Buddhist banner with a chant of devotion to the Lotus Sutra (*'Namu Myōhō Renge Kyō'*), from Takagi Takeshi's 1915 book *Comparing Eastern and Western Bushidō*. Image courtesy of the National Diet Library, Tokyo.

fleet in 1853 resulted in the placement of a permanent consul soon thereafter. This broke sharply with previous practice in Japan's international relations, and one of the great challenges for the Tokugawa rulers was to understand the new methods of diplomacy that were being standardised and imposed by the Western empires. Like China and many other Asian states before, Japan was forced to sign so-called 'unequal treaties' that gave the Western powers a wide range of unreciprocated rights and controls over their citizens and trade that passed through newly established 'treaty ports' such as Kobe and Yokohama. China's devastating defeat by Britain in the Opium Wars of 1839–42 and 1856–60 provided a stark warning to Japanese leaders of the dangers of resisting the treaties, leading the Tokugawa into a conflict with powerful domestic anti-foreign factions that ultimately led to the collapse of the shogunate.

With Japan facing a perceived existential threat from the Western powers, diplomacy was more important than it had been for several

106 *Oleg Benesch*

Figure 5.2 'Western warriors and religion', from Takagi Takeshi's 1915 book *Comparing Eastern and Western Bushidō*. Image courtesy of the National Diet Library, Tokyo.

centuries. Japanese rulers had engaged diplomatically with a highly diverse group of counterparts during the Tokugawa age, including the great Ming and Qing empires, the neighbouring kingdom of Korea, the semi-dependent Ryukyu Kingdom, the Dutch in their small factory at Nagasaki, as well as various Russian missions and the Ainu people to the north. Overall, diplomacy was largely conducted on Japan's terms, although reflecting the balances of power between the parties. Interactions with the West, however, forced Japanese leaders to quickly adapt to new standards and practices of diplomacy from a vulnerable position. At the same time, Meiji leaders also realised the utility of these practices and soon applied them to their own interactions with Korea, which they then threatened to invade due to its 'backwardness' relative to Japan.

In this context, although modern international relations were redefined by the emergence of the nation state, many diplomatic protocols and ceremonies were directly and indirectly related to European medievalism and crusader heritage, which could also conveniently dovetail with certain existing Japanese practices. These dynamics could be seen in Japanese missions to Britain, British missions to Japan, and in the influence of medievalist European notions of nobility in the construction of a modern Japanese aristocracy.[37] As the quote from the later diplomat and Undersecretary of the League of Nations, Nitobe Inazō, at the top of this section shows, these interactions were coloured throughout by martial aspects that were never far below the surface in international relations during this period.

From the 1860s, Western visitors to Japan were fascinated by castles, swords, samurai, and other accoutrements of the 'feudal' past. The perception of a shared martial medieval past was reinforced by diplomatic gifts of swords and armour, and Japanese craftsmanship in these areas had been renowned for centuries in East Asia. In turn, medievalism, including crusader heritage, could not be overlooked by diplomats and other Japanese travellers to Europe. Modern monarchs often lived in medieval castles, where they received Japanese visitors in traditional halls with attendants dressed in medievalist costume. At Windsor Castle, home to the most powerful monarch in the world, visitors were awed by the Gothic Revival embellishments such as the great expansion of the Round Tower in the 1820s and 1830s that doubled its height.[38]

Perhaps the most revealing episode in this regard is the journey of the Iwakura Mission, an unprecedented undertaking in which a large proportion of the Meiji leadership embarked on a journey of diplomacy and research around the world from 1871 to 1873. The members of the mission visited dozens of European castles at the behest of their various hosts, including – just in Britain – Beeston, Blair, Edinburgh, Finlarig, Peckforton, Rosslyn, and Warwick. In addition to calling on the queen at Windsor, the mission visited the Tower of London, already one of the top sights on the London tourist circuit. The account of the Tower of London in the mission's official record is extensive, discussing its holdings of historic swords and armour, but also the very concept of repurposing an obsolete fortification as a military museum to educate the populace about the great martial exploits of the nation; a trend that struck the Japanese observers across Europe.[39] The Iwakura delegates were also taken by the presence of Japanese swords and armour from the seventeenth century in the Tower's collection, even if they deemed these items to be of inferior quality by Japanese standards.[40]

It is important to note that the Tower of London as visited by the mission was no mere medieval relic, but had been substantially renovated and enhanced by medievalist constructions such as the Waterloo Barracks and the Regimental Headquarters of the Royal Regiment of Fusiliers, completed in the 1840s. Similarly, the Palace of Westminster was rebuilt in a Gothic style after a fire in 1834 destroyed the mix of structures that housed parliament up to that time. This mammoth project took several decades, and was only completed in 1870, shortly before the Iwakura Mission arrived in Britain.

The journey through Europe convinced the Japanese mission of the significance of religious conflict in Western history. As the official chronicler of the mission recorded:

> From the Crusades of the Middle Ages up until the Protestant revolts of early modern times, blood flowed for hundreds of years as people were massacred and cut down like reeds. More recently, when Napoleon Bonaparte invaded Russia, [...] The Russians [...] made the clergy tell the people that their foes [the French] were enemies of the Greek faith and that the fate of the Orthodox Church itself rested on the outcome.[41]

In Japan, which had not experienced major religious conflict for over two centuries, since the violent suppression of the Christian Shimabara Rebellion in 1637–38, Christian militarism seemed especially concerning. As the mission record observed, 'Looking at other wards in Europe, it is invariably religion which unites the hearts of the people, and in wars involving religion their fury is as terrifying as that of raging lions and tigers.'[42] The discourse of the Meiji period also led to a longer-term claim by some Japanese commentators that European wars such as the crusades were much more violent than Japanese wars, as the former were fought against other 'races', whereas the domestic nature of Japan's civil wars made them more tragic.[43] Coverage of international events became increasingly widely disseminated with the rapid growth of newspapers and other popular media in Japan throughout the Meiji period, while Japan's station in the world continued to rise. Throughout this time, the British Empire was the primary reference point for Japan, and Japan became increasingly important for Britain, as well, especially after victory in the Sino-Japanese War in 1895.[44]

In the context of crusader medievalism, the first decade of the new century was the most significant, as Japan and Britain concluded the Anglo-Japanese Alliance in 1902. From the 1870s, the Japanese government followed other countries in adopting court titles and diplomatic ceremonies modelled on idealised medieval European precedents in line with the developing international standards.[45] This was exemplified by the conferment of the Order of the Garter on the Meiji Emperor by King Edward VII in 1906, covered in great detail in the 280-page account by Algernon Freeman-Mitford (1837–1916), 1st Baron Redesdale, who had been stationed as a diplomat in Japan around the time of the Meiji Restoration. As Anthony Best has argued, the decision to bestow the Garter on the emperor was highly controversial for reasons of racism and religious difference, with the latter especially relevant in the case of the professed Christian ideals of the chivalric order.[46] As the prince said to the emperor during the ceremony, 'Your Majesty is no doubt aware that the Order of the Garter was instituted nearly six hundred years ago, as an Order of chivalry, by King Edward the Third, and it is recognised as our most noble Order of Knighthood', thereby explicitly tying the Garter to the medieval and crusading past.[47]

Freeman-Mitford's account was fully in keeping with the medievalist and Orientalist view of Japan common at the time. While himself witnessing a medievalesque diplomatic ceremony that drew on Britain's distant medieval legacy, when Freeman-Mitford wrote of the Japanese medieval period, he saw this as much more recent: 'By "mediaeval times" I mean the times which preceded the great Revolution of 1868.'[48] He elaborated:

> To us who are separated by centuries from the chivalry and the poetry of feudal times, these things seem remote indeed; but to the Japanese, to whom they are nearer than the days of stage-coaches and blunderbusses and Hounslow Heath are to the Englishman, they are no dream of the past, but a reality, living in a new form in the spirit of patriotism and loyalty which is their dearest inheritance.[49]

Despite the great differences in chronology, for Japanese and British leaders, the mutual recognition of one another's martial medieval past was a key component of their close relationship. In this way, the Garter Mission served to link elements of the crusades, often seen as the origins of the Order of the Garter, and the samurai spirit that had supposedly seen Japan to victory over Russia the previous year and confirmed the empire as Britain's closest ally.

Religion: baptising bushido

> Bushido is the greatest product of the Japanese nation, but bushido itself does not have the power to save Japan. Christianity grafted to the stock of bushido is the world's greatest product, and has the power to not only save the Japanese nation but the entire world.[50]
>
> (Uchimura Kanzō, 1916)

The great potential ascribed to bushido by the Protestant minister Uchimura Kanzō (1861–1930) reflects its high profile, while Uchimura's childhood friend, the Quaker Nitobe Inazō, celebrated bushido as the 'animating spirit' and 'motor force' of Japan.[51] Uchimura and Nitobe were representative of a generation of prominent Japanese Christians in the Meiji period who sought to combine their faith with samurai ideals in order to both promote Christianity in Japan and Japanese culture in the West. Due to their engagement with Christianity, which was reintroduced to Japan after having been banned from the early seventeenth century to 1873, Japanese Christians were much more closely engaged with the larger global moment of reinvention and celebration of the Middle Ages, and especially the role of the crusades and medieval knighthood.

This section focuses on Japanese Christians in the global medievalist moment, when the appropriation of samurai ideals provided patriotic legitimacy and a possibility for expanding Christian conversion, while also providing a tool for explaining Japan to foreigners through perceived commonalities. Although the mainstream bushido ideology of the time has become widely associated with Japanese militarism and traditional values, bushido was also a key vehicle for Japanese Christians to defend and disseminate their 'foreign' faith in the nationalistic and often hostile climate of the late Meiji period.[52] Christians have never exceeded one per cent of Japan's population, but have had a disproportionately large influence on the nation's cultural and intellectual life, and this includes Japanese bushido discourse. Christians simultaneously stressed the historicity of bushido as well as its compatibility with Christianity; acknowledging the recent provenance of bushido as an invented tradition would have undermined this project.

Bushido provided a religiously neutral yet patriotically sound basis for a new Japanese Christian identity, which was vital at a time of burgeoning nationalism and lingering suspicion of Christianity. Although Christianity was not banned again, the dismissal of Uchimura Kanzō from his teaching post at the First Higher School for allegedly failing to bow sufficiently to the sacred Imperial Rescript on Education in 1891 reflected the precarious position of Japanese Christians. This *lèse-majesté* incident made national headlines, further spreading distrust of Christians throughout the country.[53] In this context, bushido presented a unique opportunity, and a disproportionate number of early Japanese writers on bushido were Christians. The majority of prominent Japanese Christians felt compelled to address bushido in their writings, and some scholars have divided modern bushido discourse into two broad streams along 'nationalist' and 'Christian' lines.[54]

Many Japanese Christians were drawn to bushido out of a combination of medievalist interest and a desire for patriotic legitimacy. Bushido was a conveniently ambiguous concept that could be appropriated by Christians and other marginalised groups in an increasingly nationalistic climate in which medievalism was a significant cultural force. Nitobe hinted at this opportunity: 'One remarkable difference between the experience of Europe and of Japan is, that, whereas in Europe when Chivalry was weaned from Feudalism and was adopted by the Church, it obtained a fresh lease of life, in Japan no religion was large enough to nourish it', suggesting that this could change with the arrival of Christianity.[55]

The Tokugawa ban on missionary activity was lifted in 1873, combining with the large-scale recruitment of Western specialists for Japan's ambitious modernisation plans. Many Japanese enrolled in Western schools as foreign training and language study provided significant opportunities for advancement. Exposure to foreign ideas often included contact with Christianity, and many foreigners reinforced the notion that Western technological and institutional progress were closely linked to Western religion.[56] This could be seen in the case of the Sapporo Agricultural College, where the American principal William S. Clark (1826–1886) strongly influenced the conversion of his young students, including Uchimura, Nitobe, and many others.

While Nitobe was the writer of the most influential work on bushido outside of Japan, other Christian bushido theorists were more significant to discourse within Japan as it developed in the 1890s. Perhaps the most important was the Protestant minister Uemura Masahisa (1858–1925), who worked primarily in Japanese and pre-empted many of Nitobe's ideas, although they can both be seen as Japanese Christians within the global medievalist moment. If Nitobe endeavoured to have Japanese medievalism recognised by Western audiences, Uemura similarly outlined a medievalist heritage of a global standard to domestic Japanese audiences.

Uemura was the earliest significant Meiji Christian bushido theorist, and was one of the first thinkers to specifically use the term.

His views on the subject remained remarkably consistent, making his commentaries a useful barometer for the changes in broader bushido discourse. When Uemura felt that bushido discourse was being corrupted as it began to attract broader interest following the Sino-Japanese War, he lamented that the concept had been hijacked by nationalists.[57] Uemura's primary concern was promoting Christianity within Japan, leading him to promote elements of Western history and thought, including medievalism, while maintaining a critical stance towards contemporary Japanese society.

Uemura published two articles on bushido in his *Fukuin shinpō* (*Evangelical Weekly*) newspaper in March and June 1894, in which he sought to reconcile the supposed Japanese 'warrior spirit' with Christianity. Like Ozaki and other writers on bushido at the time, Uemura was motivated to write about bushido by the perceived decay in morality and vitality that had occurred during the first twenty-five years of Meiji: 'current society is anesthetised and lifeless as never before. Without turning to Christianity we will not be able to revive this country. At the same time, we must look to our past.'[58] While promoting what was perceived as a Western religion, Uemura joined many other Japanese thinkers of the 1890s in arguing that aspects of Westernisation were undercutting Japanese traditions and ethics, and that modernisation exacerbated this by promoting materialism and increasing feelings of inequality.[59] In other words, one of the most pressing issues facing Japan was addressing the moral vacuum that had arisen during the Meiji period.

Uemura opened his 'Christianity and Bushido' by establishing similarities between the West and Japan, and was especially interested in Europe's medieval period. Like his contemporary Ozaki, Uemura sought the foundations of Western economic and military primacy in feudal knighthood. Following the successive collapses of the Roman and Holy Roman Empires, Uemura wrote, medieval Europe was partitioned and dominated by warlike and barbarian Teutonic tribes. During this dark and isolated time:

> in feudal society another unique type of spirit was born. Fearing God and respecting man, revering the old and cherishing the young, earnestly striving for justice, this spirit did not shrink from flood or fire. Readily exposing false accusations and crushing arrogance, helping the weak and facing the strong, in turn being composed and silently praying for the emperor, offering one's life for God or the church with purpose and dedication, and especially showing loving respect to women, all of these were viewed

as being sacred. Historians have given this a name and call it chivalry. In short, this is what is known as warriors grasping a sword with the right hand and holding the Holy Scriptures in the left.[60]

Uemura's description of chivalry arising from martial Christianity reflected the dominant crusade narratives in Japan at the time, as seen in the mainstream history textbooks.

In comparison, Uemura pointed out that Japan had from ancient times been known as a martial land, and that 'the thing known as bushido is that which has come to take the most distinguished and beautiful form of the spirit that worships martiality.'[61] While claiming that bushido had existed from ancient times, Uemura saw the pinnacle of its development under the Tokugawa, when 'the vitality of society was in the samurai [bushi], and the vitality of the samurai was in bushido, while those areas of society that had bushido had the truest character and were the best regulated.' Furthermore, 'If one desires to understand European chivalry, one must not forget the influence of Christianity. If one desires to know the development of bushido, one must not forget the amount of strength that Buddhism and Confucianism contributed.'[62] However, Uemura contended, when feudal society collapsed, Buddhism and Confucianism collapsed with it, and even the remnants of bushido were in the process of being buried, for when the samurai put away their swords and bows, they also consigned bushido to the past. Uemura lamented the demise of bushido, this 'beautiful flower of the human mind' which had been nurtured by the Japanese people for hundreds of years.[63] Uemura called upon his countrymen to not stand idly by while the nation's spiritual inheritance from the warrior class disintegrated or, even worse, was intentionally expunged from society. 'Bushido', he argued, 'is truly like a type of religion, and society was able to maintain its life through it [...] Society must revive the old bushido. Or rather, what I desire is a bushido that has received the baptism.'[64] Drawing on both Christianity and Japan's own martial past, Uemura proposed the conversion of Japan to Christianity.[65]

Uemura's laments concerning the decline of bushido from its medieval ideal echoed contemporary European concerns. A core aspect of the medievalist revival in the nineteenth century was the notion that chivalry had declined from an earlier ideal and needed to be consciously resurrected. This discourse was picked up by Japanese thinkers, including Nitobe, who wrote, 'The particular and local causes for the decay of Chivalry which St. Palaye gives, have, of course, little application to Japanese conditions; but the larger and more general causes that helped to undermine Knighthood and Chivalry in and after the Middle Ages are as surely working for the decline of Bushido.'⁶⁶ The work in question was *Mémoires sur l'ancienne chevalerie,* first published in 1759 by French historian Jean-Baptiste de la Curne de Sainte-Palaye (1697–1781), who influentially discussed the origins and influences of crusading and chivalry on European 'civilisation' and strengthened associations between the two.⁶⁷

The decline of feudalism in Japan left bushido 'an orphan', and unable to be sustained by Shinto, Confucianism, or secular institutions. For European thinkers, Japan was an example of a society that had maintained its medieval chivalric heritage even as their own had declined.⁶⁸ As Arthur May Knapp wrote in 1896, to people in Japan, the samurai represented 'the same lofty virtues and heroic devotion which we associate with the truest knight of Mediaeval Romance', and that the 'knightly virtue' of the samurai 'has escaped the degeneration which it has suffered in Europe, and has remained to this day a stainless glory.'⁶⁹ For many Japanese thinkers, the opposite was true: Europe had preserved its knightly virtues even as samurai traditions were being lost. The grass tended to seem greener on the other side.

Conclusions

Adrian Pinnington has suggested that Japanese Christians were attracted to bushido due to a sense of nostalgia and the potential for comparison with European chivalry.⁷⁰ The influence of nostalgia in Meiji Japan should not be underestimated, but it must be noted that it went beyond Christians and arguably had a greater effect on many other segments of society.⁷¹ The widespread interest in chivalry was certainly reflected in works by Christians and non-Christians alike, at least until the turn of the century. In the midst of the global medievalist moment, we can see how a parallel Japanese medievalism sought to identify a local 'medieval' past, create an indigenous version of chivalry in the form of bushido, and to see samurai warriors as occupying the same place within this system as crusader knights came to occupy in nineteenth-century Europe – namely as embodiments and paragons of this cultural project.

After 1900, however, as the environment became considerably more nationalistic, bushido discourse also became more chauvinistic. There was a dramatic change in the previous position of the West as primarily a model for Japan to emulate, and this included views of chivalry and the crusades. While Uemura had emphasised that part of chivalry was 'showing loving respect to women', the right-wing philosopher Inoue Tetsujirō attacked European chivalry as mere 'woman-worship' that was vastly inferior to bushido, and these disparaging views were even repeated by some Japanese Christians.[72] Although Christian thinkers continued to write about bushido and chivalry, their views were relegated to the margins as an emperor-centred 'imperial bushido' ideology became dominant. Even Nitobe's heavily Christian-influenced *Bushido: The Soul of Japan*, which became a global bestseller in the first decade of the twentieth century, was widely criticised by Inoue and other commentators to the extent that Nitobe resisted its translation into Japanese until after the Russo-Japanese War, and it had limited impact on Japanese bushido discourse.

As in Europe, the crusades and chivalry were influential in Japan until the First World War. While earlier historians located the death of medievalism in the mechanised and industrialised warfare of the Great War, more recent scholarship has shown that medievalist trends in the West continued well into the interwar period and even until 1945. This is certainly the case in Japan, where medievalism remained strong until defeat in 1945. That said, Japanese medievalism underwent a significant shift around the time of the First World War, and Western chivalry was largely displaced from popular discourse by nativist Japanese models based on the samurai and bushido. At the same time, the interwar period also saw the first substantial original research by Japanese scholars on European medieval history, and only in the 1960s did crusades research in Japan become an established field.[73] Having first contributed to internationalising chivalry and the crusades in the late nineteenth century, Japan followed an established pattern in nationalising its medieval history as it moved into the twentieth.

Notes

1. I am very grateful to Mike Horswell and Ran Zwigenberg for their detailed comments on various versions of this chapter.
2. Horswell, *British Crusader Medievalism*.
3. Ibid., pp. 11–16.
4. Ronnie Ellenblum, *Crusader Castles and Modern History* (Cambridge, 2007), pp. 3–4; Knobler, 'Holy Wars'.
5. Basil Hall Chamberlain, *Things Japanese* (London, 1891), p. 1.
6. For example, Mark Girouard, *The Return to Camelot* (London, 1981); Elizabeth Emery and Laura Morowitz, *Consuming the Past* (Aldershot, 2003); Stefan Goebel, *The Great War and Medieval Memory* (Cambridge, 2007); Patrick J. Geary, and Gábor Klaniczay (eds.), *Manufacturing the Middle Ages* (Leiden, 2013).
7. Kathleen Davis and Nadia Altschul, *Medievalisms in the Postcolonial World* (Baltimore, MD, 2009).
8. See, for example, the special issue of *Past & Present* on *Towards a Global Middle Ages*, edited by Catherine Holmes and Naomi Standen (Vol. 238, November 2018).

9 See the introduction to this volume, and Amanda Behm, *Imperial History and the Global Politics of Exclusion* (London, 2018), pp. 11–17, 33, 201.
10 For a comparative discussion of this dynamic, see Margrit Pernau et al., *Civilizing Emotions* (Oxford, 2015).
11 Jonathan Phillips, *The Life and Legend of the Sultan Saladin* (London, 2019), p. 344.
12 Ahmet A. Ersoy, *Architecture and the Late Ottoman Historical Imaginary* (Surrey, 2015).
13 Ram Sharan Sharma, *Early Medieval Indian Society* (Hyderabad, India, 2001); Daud Ali, 'The Idea of the Medieval in the Writing of South Asian History: Contexts, Methods and Politics', *Social History* 39 (2014), pp. 382–407.
14 Joachim Kurtz, 'Chinese Dreams of the Middle Ages: Nostalgia, Utopia, Propaganda', *The Medieval History Journal* 21 (2018), p. 6.
15 There is insufficient space here to discuss the complex problems inherent in the term 'feudal', the use of which has been persuasively challenged with regard to European history as well (Susan Reynolds, *Fiefs and Vassals* (Oxford, 1994)). This study uses the concept as it was commonly cited by Meiji writers on *bushidō*, many of whom directly transposed a nineteenth-century European understanding of medieval society onto Japanese historical models.
16 John W. Hall, 'Feudalism in Japan – A Reassessment', *Comparative Studies in Society and History* 5 (1962), pp. 15–51; Karl F. Friday, 'The Futile Paradigm: In Quest of Feudalism in Early Medieval Japan', *History Compass* 8 (2010), pp. 179–96.
17 Oleg Benesch and Ran Zwigenberg, *Japan's Castles* (Cambridge, 2019).
18 Japanese names in this study are given in the traditional order, with the family name first. Fukuzawa is the family name, and Yukichi is the given name. Yatsuzuka, 'Jūjigun kotohajime', p. 70.
19 Ibid., pp. 70–75.
20 Ibid, p. 77.
21 William Cooke Taylor, Kimura Ippo trans. *Bankoku shi Volume 3* (Tokyo, 1878), pp. 387–454 deal with the crusades. Yatsuzuka, 'Jūjigun kotohajime', p. 82.
22 Yatsuzuka Shunji, 'Nihon ni okeru jūjigun kenkyū 1: Meiji jidai kōhan', *Shiyū* 9 (2001), p. 33.
23 Taylor, *Manual*, p. 428.
24 Ibid., p. 30.
25 Yatsuzuka, 'Jūjigun kotohajime', p. 81.
26 Samuel Goodrich, *Peter Parley's Universal History on the Basis of Geography* (New York, 1850), pp. 35–36.
27 Samuel Goodrich, *Pārē bankoku shi Volume 2*, trans. Makiyama Kōhei (Tokyo, 1876), p. 29.
28 Taylor, *Bankoku shi,* pp. 448–50. Taylor, *Manual*, p. 429.
29 Shunji, 'Nihon ni okeru jūjigun kenkyū 1', p. 40.
30 For an examination of this process, see: Thomas Keirstead, 'Inventing Medieval Japan: The History and Politics of National Identity', *The Medieval History Journal* 1 (1998), pp. 47–71.

31 See, for example: Karl F. Friday, 'Bushidō or Bull? A Medieval Historian's Perspective on the Imperial Army and the Japanese Warrior Tradition', *The History Teacher* 27 (1994), pp. 339–49; Oleg Benesch, *Inventing the Way of the Samurai* (Oxford, 2014).
32 Ozaki Yukio, 'Shinshi (Gentleman)', *Ozaki Gakudō zenshū Vol. 3* (Tokyo, 1955), pp. 743–48; Ozaki Yukio, 'Bushidō', *Naichi gaikō* (Tokyo, 1893), pp. 25–28.
33 Benesch, *Inventing*, chapters 4–6.
34 Nitobe Inazō, *Bushido: The Soul of Japan* (Tokyo, 1908), p. 167.
35 Takagi Takeshi. *Tōzai bushidō no hikaku*. Tokyo: Tsūzoku Tosho Chūō Hanbaijo, 1915, pp. 122–23. Figure 5.1 was originally created by Alphonse-Marie-Adolphe de Neuville (1835–85) and appeared on p. 371 of François Guizot's (1787–1874) *L'histoire de France depuis les temps les plus reculés jusqu'en 1789, racontée à mes petits enfants, vol. 1* (Paris: Librairie Hachette, 1872). The book was translated into English c.1883. I'm grateful to Mike Horswell for this reference.
36 Nitobe, *Bushido*, p. 9.
37 John Breen, 'The Rituals of Anglo-Japanese Diplomacy: Imperial Audiences in Early Meiji Japan', in *The History of Anglo-Japanese Relations 1600–2000*, eds. G. Daniels and C. Tsuzuki (London, 2002) pp. 60–76.
38 Girouard, *Return to Camelot*, pp. 26–27.
39 Kume Kunitake ed., *The Iwakura Embassy 1871–73: A True Account of the Ambassador Extraordinary & Plenipotentiary's Journey of Observation Through the United States of America and Europe (Volume III, Continental Europe, 1)*, trans. Andrew Cobbing (Princeton, NJ, 2002), p. 328.
40 Kume Kunitake ed., *The Iwakura Embassy 1871–73: (Volume II, Britain)*, trans. Graham Healey (Princeton, NJ, 2002), p. 97.
41 Kume Kunitake ed. *The Iwakura Embassy 1871–73: (Volume III, Continental Europe, 1)*, trans. Andrew Cobbing (Princeton, NJ, 2002), p. 237.
42 Ibid.
43 Benesch, *Inventing*, p. 190.
44 Cees Heere, *Empire Ascendant* (Oxford, 2020), pp. 13–18.
45 Breen, 'Anglo-Japanese Diplomacy'.
46 Antony Best, 'Race, Monarchy, and the Anglo-Japanese Alliance, 1902–1922', *Social Science Japan Journal* 9 (2006), pp. 178–80.
47 Algernon Freeman-Mitford, *The Garter Mission to Japan* (London, 1906), pp. 17–21.
48 Ibid., p. 89.
49 Ibid., pp. 90–91.
50 Uchimura Kanzō, 'Untitled', *Seisho no kenkyū*, 186 (1916); reproduced in Matsumae Shigeyoshi, *Budō shisō no tankyū* (Tokyo, 1987), p. 91.
51 Nitobe, *Bushido*, p. 179.
52 Benesch, *Inventing*, pp. 140–47.
53 John F. Howes, *Japan's Modern Prophet: Uchimura Kanzo 1861–1930* (Vancouver, BC, 2005), pp. 4, 70–77.
54 Kanno Kakumyō, *Bushidō no gyakushū* (Tokyo, 2004), pp. 260–61; Unoda Shōya, 'Bushidō ron no seiritsu: Seiyō to Tōyō no aida', *Edo no shisō 7 (shisō shi no 19 seiki)* (Tokyo, 1997), pp. 29–50; Funatsu Akio,

'Meiji ki no bushidō ni tsuite no ichi kōsatsu: Nitobe Inazō *Bushidō* wo chūshin ni', *Kotoba to bunka* 4 (2003), p. 24; Matsumae Shigeyoshi, *Budō shisō no tankyū* (Tōkai Daigaku Shuppankai, 1987).
55 Nitobe, *Bushido*, p. 167.
56 Helen Ballhatchet, 'The Religion of the West versus the Science of the West: The Evolution Controversy in Late Nineteenth Century Japan', in *Japan and Christianity*, eds. John Breen and Mark Williams (London, 1996), pp. 109–10.
57 Uemura Masahisa, 'Kirisutokyō no bushidō', *Uemura Masahisa chosakushū Volume 1* (Tokyo, 1966). pp. 398–404.
58 Ibid., p. 396.
59 Ashina Sadamichi, 'Uemura Masahisa no Nihonron (1): kindai Nihon to Kirisutokyō', *Ajia/Kirisutokyō/tagensei 6* (March 2008), pp. 7–8.
60 Uemura, 'Kirisuto kyō to bushidō', pp. 391–92.
61 Ibid., pp. 393.
62 Ibid., pp. 394.
63 Ibid.
64 Ibid., pp. 394–95.
65 Uemura Masahisa, 'Nani wo motte bushidō no sui wo hozon sen to suru ka', in *Uemura Masahisa chosakushū*, vol. 1 (Tokyo, 1966), pp. 397–98.
66 Nitobe, *Bushido*, p. 167.
67 Tyerman, *Debate*, pp. 73–77.
68 Colin Holmes, and A.H. Ion, 'Bushido and the Samurai: Images in British Public Opinion, 1894–1914' *Modern Asian Studies* 14 (1980), pp. 309–29; Chika Tonooka, 'Reverse Emulation and the Cult of Japanese Efficiency in Edwardian Britain', *The Historical Journal* 60 (2017), pp. 95–119.
69 Arthur May Knapp, *Feudal and Modern Japan* (Boston, MA, 1898), pp. 49–51.
70 Adrian Pinnington, 'Introduction', in *Critical Readings on Japan, 1906–1948*, vol. 1, ed. Peter O'Connor (Tokyo, 2008), p. xxxvii.
71 For a case study of nostalgia in Meiji, see Carol Gluck, 'The Invention of Edo', in *Mirror of Modernity*, ed. Stephen Vlastos (Oakland, CA, 1998), pp. 262–84.
72 Inoue, *Bushidō*, pp. 6–7; John Toshimichi Imai, *Bushido in the Past and Present* (Tokyo, 1906), p. 69. Sarah Thal has put forward a compelling argument that many conservative bushido theorists saw the lack of respect for women in the samurai ethic, relative to European chivalry, as a point of pride and strength: <https://meijiat150.podbean.com/e/episode-45-dr-sarah-thal-wisconsin/> [accessed 18 April 2022].
73 Yatsuzuka. 'Nihon ni okeru jūjigun kenkyū 1', p. 23.

Bibliography

Primary

Chamberlain, Basil Hall. *Things Japanese*. London: Kegan Paul, 1891.
Freeman-Mitford, Algernon. *The Garter Mission to Japan*. London: MacMillan and Co., 1906.

Goodrich, Samuel. *Peter Parley's Universal History on the Basis of Geography*. New York: Newman, 1850.

———. *Pārē bankoku shi Volume 2*. Trans. Makiyama Kōhei. Tokyo: Monbushō, 1876.

Imai, John Toshimichi. *Bushido in the Past and Present*. Tokyo: Kanazashi, 1906.

Kanzō, Uchimura. 'Untitled'. In *Seisho no kenkyū* 186 (1916). *Budō shisō no tankyū*. Ed. Matsumae Shigeyoshi. Tokyo: Tōkai Daigaku Shuppankai, 1987, p. 91.

Knapp, Arthur May. *Feudal and Modern Japan*. Boston, MA: Joseph Knight Company, 1898.

Kume Kunitake, ed. *The Iwakura Embassy 1871–73: A True Account of the Ambassador Extraordinary & Plenipotentiary's Journey of Observation Through the United States of America and Europe (Volume III, Continental Europe, 1)*. Trans. Andrew Cobbing. Princeton, NJ: Princeton University Press, 2002.

———. ed. *The Iwakura Embassy 1871–73: A True Account of the Ambassador Extraordinary & Plenipotentiary's Journey of Observation Through the United States of America and Europe (Volume II, Britain)*. Trans. Graham Healey. Princeton, NJ: Princeton University Press, 2002.

Nitobe, Inazō. *Bushido: The Soul of Japan*. Tokyo: Teibi, 1908.

Ozaki Yukio. 'Bushidō'. *Naichi gaikō*. Tokyo: Hakubundō, 1893, pp. 25–28.

———. '*Shinshi* (Gentleman)'. *Ozaki Gakudō zenshū Vol. 3*. Tokyo: Kōronsha, 1955. pp. 743–48.

Takagi Takeshi. *Tōzai bushidō no hikaku*. Tokyo: Tsūzoku Tosho Chūō Hanbaijo, 1915.

Taylor, William Cooke. *Bankoku shi Volume 3*. Trans. Kimura Ippo. Tokyo: Monbushō Henshū Kyoku, 1878.

Uemura Masahisa. 'Kirisutokyō no bushidō'. In *Uemura Masahisa chosakushū Volume 1*. Eds. Ishihara Ken, Kumano Yoshitaka, Ōuchi Saburō and Saitō Takeshi. Tokyo: Shinkyō Shuppansha, 1966, pp. 398–404.

———. 'Nani wo motte bushidō no sui wo hozon sen to suru ka'. In *Uemura Masahisa chosakushū Volume 1*. Eds. Ishihara Ken, Kumano Yoshitaka, Ōuchi Saburō and Saitō Takeshi. Tokyo: Shinkyō Shuppansha, 1966, pp. 396–97.

Secondary

Ali, Daud. 'The Idea of the Medieval in the Writing of South Asian History: Contexts, Methods and Politics', *Social History* 39 (2014), pp. 382–407.

Ballhatchet, Helen. 'The Religion of the West versus the Science of the West: The Evolution Controversy in Late Nineteenth Century Japan'. In *Japan and Christianity: Impacts and Responses*. Eds. John Breen and Mark Williams. London: Macmillan Press, 1996, pp. 107–21.

Behm, Amanda. *Imperial History and the Global Politics of Exclusion: Britain, 1880–1940*. London: Palgrave Macmillan, 2018.

Benesch, Oleg. *Inventing the Way of the Samurai: Nationalism, Internationalism, and Bushido in Modern Japan*. Oxford: OUP, 2014.

Benesch, Oleg and Ran Zwigenberg. *Japan's Castles: Citadels of Modernity in War and Peace*. Cambridge: CUP, 2019.
Best, Antony. 'Race, Monarchy, and the Anglo-Japanese Alliance, 1902–1922'. *Social Science Japan Journal* 9 (2006), pp. 171–86.
Breen, John. 'The Rituals of Anglo-Japanese Diplomacy: Imperial Audiences in Early Meiji Japan'. In *The History of Anglo-Japanese Relations 1600–2000*. Eds. G. Daniels and C. Tsuzuki. London: Palgrave Macmillan, 2002, pp. 60–76.
Davis, Kathleen and Nadia Altschul. *Medievalisms in the Postcolonial World: The Idea of the 'Middle Ages' Outside Europe*. Baltimore, MD: Johns Hopkins University Press, 2009.
Ellenblum, Ronnie. *Crusader Castles and Modern History*. Cambridge: CUP, 2007.
Emery, Elizabeth, and Laura Morowitz. *Consuming the Past: The Medieval Revival in Fin-de-siècle France*. Aldershot: Ashgate, 2003.
Ersoy, Ahmet A. *Architecture and the Late Ottoman Historical Imaginary: Reconfiguring the Architectural Past in a Modernizing Empire*. Surrey: Ashgate, 2015.
Friday, Karl F. 'Bushidō or Bull? A Medieval Historian's Perspective on the Imperial Army and the Japanese Warrior Tradition'. *The History Teacher* 27 (1994), pp. 339–49.
———. 'The Futile Paradigm: In Quest of Feudalism in Early Medieval Japan'. *History Compass* 8 (2010), pp. 179–96.
Funatsu Akio. 'Meiji ki no bushidō ni tsuite no ichi kōsatsu: Nitobe Inazō *Bushidō* wo chūshin ni'. *Kotoba to bunka* 4 (2003), pp. 17–32.
Geary, Patrick J. and Gábor Klaniczay eds. *Manufacturing the Middle Ages: Entangled History of Medievalism in Nineteenth-Century Europe*. Leiden: Brill, 2013.
Girouard, Mark. *The Return to Camelot: Chivalry and the English Gentleman*. London: Yale University Press, 1981.
Gluck, Carol. 'The Invention of Edo'. In *Mirror of Modernity: Invented Traditions in Modern Japan*. Ed. Stephen Vlastos. Oakland, CA: University of California Press, 1998, pp. 262–84.
Goebel, Stefan, *The Great War and Medieval Memory: War, Remembrance and Medievalism in Britain and Germany, 1914–1940*. Cambridge: CUP, 2007.
Hall, John W. 'Feudalism in Japan – A Reassessment'. *Comparative Studies in Society and History* 5 (1962), pp. 15–51.
Heere, Cees. *Empire Ascendant: The British World, Race, and the Rise of Japan*. Oxford: OUP, 2020.
Holmes, Colin and A.H. Ion. 'Bushido and the Samurai: Images in British Public Opinion, 1894–1914'. *Modern Asian Studies* 14 (1980), pp. 309–29.
Horswell, Mike. *The Rise and Fall of British Crusader Medievalism, c.1825–1945*. Abingdon: Routledge, 2018.
Howes, John F. *Japan's Modern Prophet: Uchimura Kanzo 1861–1930*. Vancouver, BC: University of British Columbia Press, 2005.

Kanno Kakumyō. *Bushidō no gyakushū*. Tokyo: Kōdansha Gendai Shinsho, 2004.
Keirstead, Thomas. 'Inventing Medieval Japan: The History and Politics of National Identity'. *The Medieval History Journal* 1 (1998), pp. 47–71.
Knobler, Adam. 'Holy Wars, Empires, and the Portability of the Past: The Modern Uses of Medieval Crusades'. *Comparative Studies in Society and History* 48 (2006), pp. 293–325.
Kurtz, Joachim. 'Chinese Dreams of the Middle Ages: Nostalgia, Utopia, Propaganda'. *The Medieval History Journal* 21 (2018), pp. 1–24.
Matsumae Shigeyoshi. *Budō shisō no tankyū*. Tokyo: Tōkai Daigaku Shuppankai, 1987.
Pernau, Margrit, Helge Jordheim, Orit Bashkin, Christian Bailey, Oleg Benesch, Jan Ifversen, Mana Kia, Rochona Majumdar, Angelika C. Messner, Myoung-kyu Park, Emmanuelle Saada, Mohinder Singh, and Einar Wigen. *Civilizing Emotions: Concepts in Nineteenth Century Europe and Asia*. Oxford: OUP, 2015.
Phillips, Jonathan. *The Life and Legend of the Sultan Saladin*. London: Bodley Head, 2019.
Pinnington, Adrian. 'Introduction'. In *Critical Readings on Japan, 1906–1948: Countering Japan's Agenda in East Asia*. Vol. 1. Ed. Peter O'Connor. Tokyo: Edition Synapse, 2008.
Reynolds, Susan. *Fiefs and Vassals: The Medieval Evidence Reinterpreted*, Oxford: OUP, 1994.
Sadamichi, Ashina. 'Uemura Masahisa no Nihonron (1): kindai Nihon to Kirisutokyō'. *Ajia/Kirisutokyō/tagensei 6*. Kyoto: Gendai Kirisutokyō Shisō Kenkyūkai, 2008, pp. 1–24.
Sharma, Ram Sharan. *Early Medieval Indian Society: A Study in Feudalisation*. Hyderabad, India: Orient Longman, 2001.
Shōya, Unoda. 'Bushidō ron no seiritsu: Seiyō to Tōyō no aida'. *Edo no shisō 7 (shisō shi no 19 seiki)*. Tokyo: Perikansha, 1997, pp. 29–50.
Tyerman, Christopher, *The Debate on the Crusades, 1099–2010*. Manchester: MUP, 2013.
Yatsuzuka Shunji. 'Jūjigun kotohajime: Nihon ni okeru 'jūjigun' no tōjō'. *Shiyū* 8 (1999), pp. 69–89.
———. 'Nihon ni okeru jūjigun kenkyū 1: Meiji jidai kōhan'. *Shiyū* 9 (2001), pp. 23–49.

Index

Abbas, Assad 78, 88–89
Afonso Henriques of Portugal 21, 23–24, 27–28, 30–33, 37, 39; sword of 27, 33
Aljubarrota, Battle of 23–24
'Athlit (castle) 4, 58–70; colony of 62, 64–65, 67

Baldwin, Stanley 1
Ben Zvi, Yitzhak 66–67, 69
Bey, Munir 78, 85–87; *see also* Evcaf
Brawer. Abraham J. 64–65
Britain: and the crusades 1, 10–12; relationship with Portugal 38; relationship with Japan 107–109
British Mandate of Palestine 59–60, 63, 65, 67–68, 84
bushido 4, 110–115

Carmona, Óscar 27
Casimiro, Augusto 30, 32
castles: British 107–108; crusader 61–62, 65, 83, 86; Japanese 102–103, 107; Portuguese 24, 27–28; of São Jorge 27–28; *see also* 'Athlit; Crac des Chevaliers
Catherine the Great of Russia 46
Catholicism: adherents 8, 83; character of Portuguese nation 25; Church 8, 28; vs Orthodoxy 47
Charles X of France 2
chivalry 99, 103–104, 109, 112–115
Ciriaci, Pietro 32
clash of civilisations 8, 11, 103
collective memory 5–7, 11

Comte, Auguste 23
Crac des Chevaliers 11, 78, 82–83, 88; *see also* Abbas, Assad
Crimean War 47, 50
crusades 1, 2–4, 7–12, 23, 38, 47, 51, 58, 60, 63–64, 66, 69, 77, 81–84, 89, 90, 98–99, 101–103, 108–109, 114–115; nationalisation of 1–2, 4–5, 11–12, 76–78, 82, 98; *see also* First Crusade; Second Crusade; Third Crusade
Cyprus 78, 82, 84, 86–87; *see also* Evcaf; Famagusta; Jeffrey, George

Dantas, Júlio 21, 31
de Oliveira, José Augusto 32
Deschamps, Paul 78, 83–84, 88–89
Dostoyevki, Fyodor 48
du Sault, Jean 29

Eighth Centenary of the Conquest of Lisbon 4, 21–22, 26–39
Enlart, Camille 83–84, 88
Erdmann, Carl 39
Estado Novo 22, 24, 26–28, 30, 37–39
Evcaf 78, 82, 85–88

Famagusta 78, 82, 84–85, 87–88
far-right 3, 11, 89
feudalism 111–112
First Crusade 9, 60
First World War 11, 30, 47–48, 50, 65, 98–99. 101, 115
France 2; and the crusades 10–12; *see also* French Mandate of Syria; Versailles, Palace of

Franco, Francisco 8
French Mandate of Syria 83–84

Great War *see* First World War
Guibert of Nogent 9

Henry the Navigator 23–24
Hissin, Haim 62
Hobsbawm, E.J. 6, 22
Hospitallers 2, 11, 46, 51, 77, 80–81; *see also* Rhodes

Islamic State (IS/ISIS/ISIL/Daesh) 3, 89
Italo-Turkish War 79–80
Iwakura Mission 107–108

Japan: foreign relations 104–109; *see also* Iwakura Mission; national identity
Jeffrey, George 78, 82–88
Jewish Palestinian Exploration Society 64–66

Kantor, Kalman Shlomo 61–62
Karo, Georg 78–82
Knights of St. John *see* Hospitallers
Knights of the Temple *see* Templars
Krak des Chevaliers *see* Crac des Chevaliers

League of Nations 11; *see also* British Mandate of Palestine; French Mandate of Syria
Lindos 78–79, 81
Lisbon 21–24, 26–30; conquest of 22–23, 28–39; *see also* Eighth Centenary of the Conquest of Lisbon
Louis IX of France 10
Louis Philippe of France 2

Malta 46, 84
Mandatory Palestine *see* British Mandate of Palestine
Mandatory Syria *see* French Mandate of Syria
Martins, Francisco da Rocha 30
Martins, Joaquim Pedro de Oliveira 29

medievalism 4, 8, 11–12, 65, 98–102, 107–108, 111–112, 115; crusader 4, 7, 10, 12, 65
Mediterranean 3–4, 77–78, 101; British and French intervention in 11, 76; *see also* British Mandate of Palestine; Cyprus; French Mandate of Syria; Malta; Rhodes
Meysels, Theodor F. 58, 68–70
military orders 10; *see also* Hospitallers; Templars; Teutonic knights
Moghabghab, Theophilus 85
Munier, Mehmed *see* Bey, Munir

national identity 5–6, 8, 61, 69, 99, 102; and heritage 83
nationalism 3, 5, 10, 81; Greek 87; Japanese 99, 102; methodological 6–7, 12; Portuguese 38; Zionist (*see* Zionism)
nations 5–6, 8, 12
Newbolt, Henry 1–2
Nicholas II, Tsar of Russia 48, 50
Nitobe, Inazō 104, 107, 110–111, 113, 115

O'Malley, Owen St Clair 29
Ottoman Empire 45–47, 76, 80, 83–84, 86, 101
Ourique, Battle of 23–24
Ozaki Yukio 104, 112

Paul I, Tsar of Russia 46, 51
Pereira, Nuno Álvares 23–24
Pernier, Luigi 78–82
Philpot, Glyn 1–2
Pitões, Pedro 31
Portugal: character of 29, 37–38; foreign relations 29–30, 37–38; perceptions of the crusades 4, 21–39
Prawer, Joshua 60
Press, Yeshayahu 64–65

Richard, Jean 2, 7, 9
Richard I, 'the Lionheart' 1, 10, 82
Rhodes 78–79
Rodrigues, Urbano 29

Russia: civil war 50; idea of the restoration of Byzantium 46; perspectives on the crusades 4, 10–11, 45; war with Japan 50
Russo-Turkish War 47

Saint Louis *see* Louis IX of France
Saladin 82, 101
Salazar, António de Oliveira 25–27
samurai 99–104, 109–110, 113–115
Saramago, José 22
Second Crusade 21–22, 29–30, 37; *see also* Lisbon, conquest of
Second World War 30, 89
Sequeira, Gustavo de Matos 32
Sino-Japanese War 108, 112

Templars 11, 58–59, 64, 66, 68; neo- 3; *see also* 'Athlit; Crac des Chevaliers
Teutonic knights 10

Third Crusade 1, 10, 82
Trevelyan, G.M. 1
Trump, Donald 11

Uchimura Kanzō 110–111
Uemura Masahisa 111–114

van der Elst, Joseph 29
Venerable Order of St. John 81, 85; *see also* Hospitallers
Versailles, Palace of 2

World War I *see* First World War
World War II *see* Second World War

Zichron Ya'akov 60–63, 65
Zionism 58–60, 64, 69; colonies 59, 62, 64 (*see also* 'Athlit; Zichron Ya'akov); perceptions of the crusades 58–60; writings 58–70; Zionism-crusade analogy 60–61

For Product Safety Concerns and Information please contact our EU representative GPSR@taylorandfrancis.com
Taylor & Francis Verlag GmbH, Kaufingerstraße 24, 80331 München, Germany

www.ingramcontent.com/pod-product-compliance
Lightning Source LLC
Chambersburg PA
CBHW051752230426
43670CB00012B/2258